An Encyclopedia of Bad Drivers

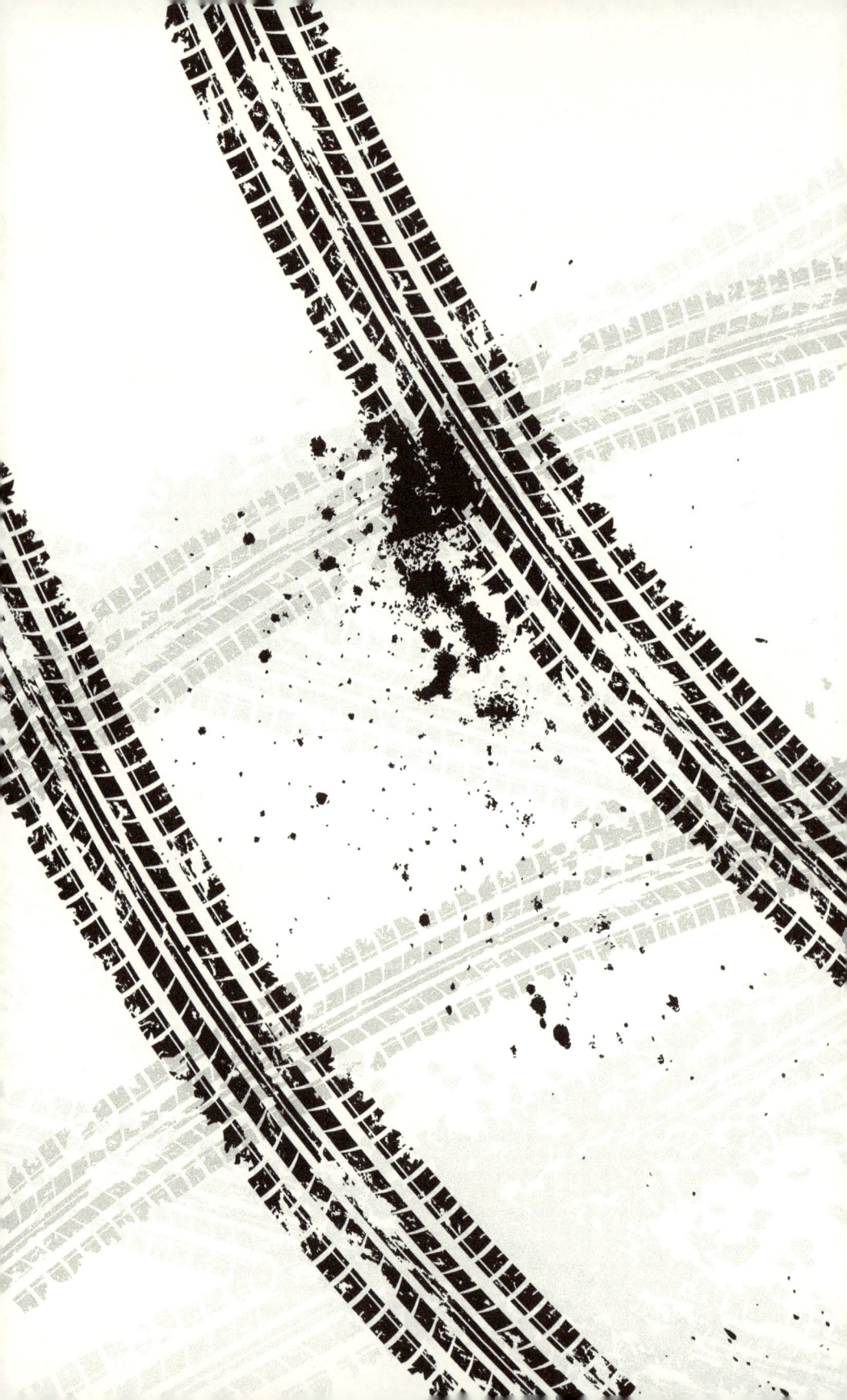

An Encyclopedia of Bad Drivers

JJ McMoon

Cover Design and
Inside Graphics by
Anthony deVito

An Encyclopedia of Bad Drivers © copyright 2018 by JJ McMoon. All rights reserved. No part of this book may be reproduced in any form whatsoever, by photography or xerography or by any other means, by broadcast or transmission, by translation into any kind of language, nor by recording electronically or otherwise, without permission in writing from the author, except by a reviewer, who may quote brief passages in critical articles or reviews.

ISBN: 978-0-692-07709-2

Printed in the United States of America
First Printing: 2018
22 21 20 19 18   5 4 3 2 1

Cover design by Anthony deVito

Virtual Everything Press
www.virtualeverything.com

Contents

	Introduction xi	
Chapter 1	All-Around Shitty Drivers 1	
Chapter 2	The Fucking Jack Asses Who Drive Slowly in the Left Lane 59	
Chapter 3	Merging Morons 65	
Chapter 4	Toll Booth Idiots 73	
Chapter 5	A Lesson in Parking Ettiquette 77	
Chapter 6	Idiots in the Snow 87	
Chapter 7	Communication 95	
Chapter 8	Aggressive Driving and Road Rage 103	
	Epilogue 115	

Also by JJ McMoon

Lives - Perception is Reality

Plan 9 From Outer Space - The Adaptation!

Plan 9 from Outer Space - The Prequel!

For my Mother,
who taught me how to drive.

Disclaimer

This book is for ENTERTAINMENT PURPOSES ONLY and in no way is intended as an instruction manual for how to drive. In fact, if you drive using some of the tactics described in this book, you will most likely find yourself in jail or worse. This is especially true for young new drivers. Please take a driver's safety course and drive defensively for a few years. Then, when your parents think you are mature enough to understand the difference between the dangers of actually operating a 2+ ton hunk of metal at dangerous speeds in a crowd of other speeding hunks of metal, and the parody of angry, completely illegal (but hopefully comedic) descriptions in this book of how to do so in a fantasy-world, feel free to read this and laugh.

Please be safe on the roads. Please live, so that you may read more books.

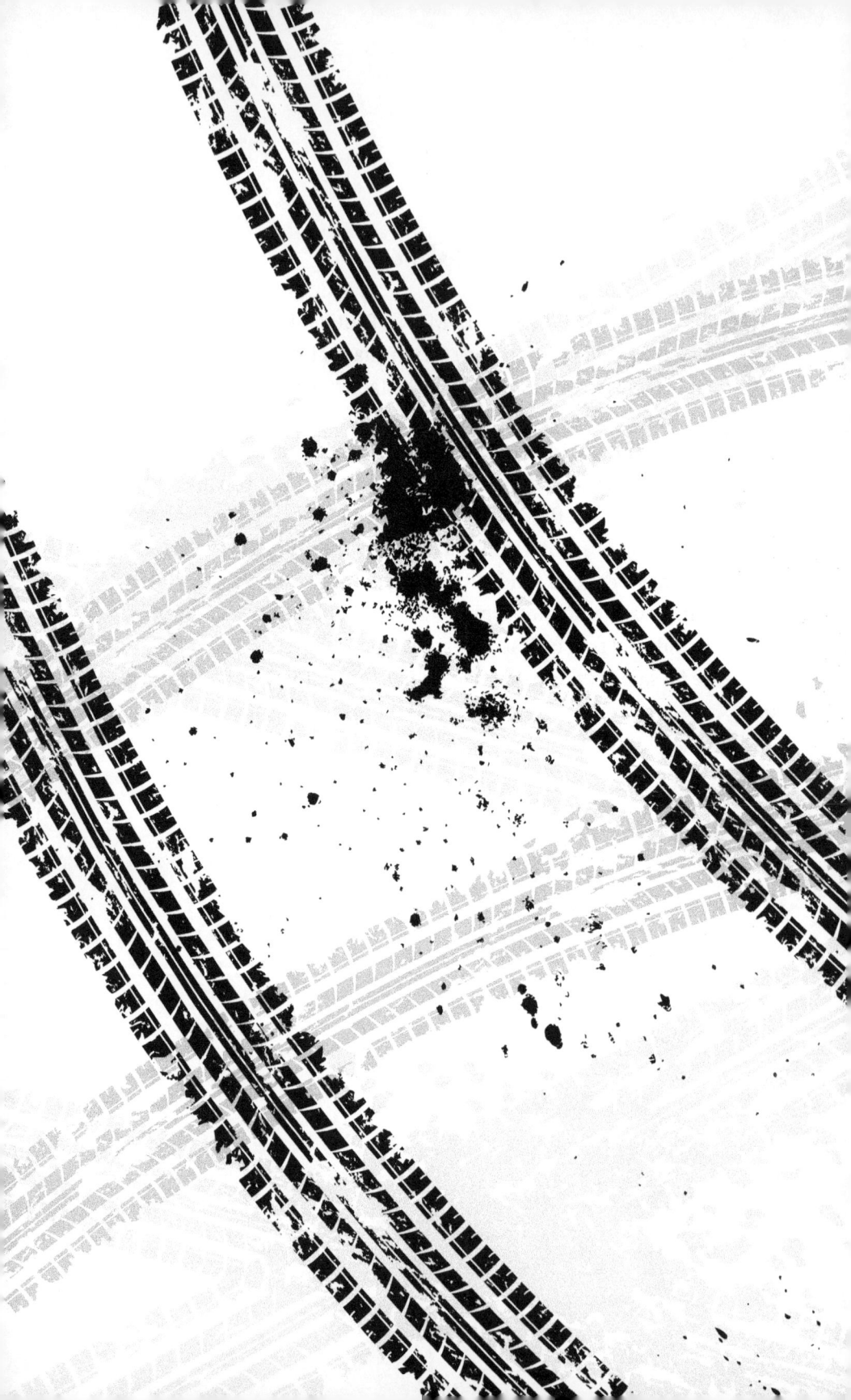

Introduction

We've all been there, haven't we? Whether it's a bad day at the office, or a fight with the wife, or too much time around a colicky baby, at some point or another we've all gotten behind the wheel with too much adrenaline. And because of the multitudes of drivers who don't go as fast as we want to, or turn when we want them to, or get out of our fucking way when we want them to ...

It can often feel like the world is populated only with idiots.

This book is for entertainment purposes only. It is profane and downright angry at times, but it was written to help you laugh at the drivers you've encountered, both outside and inside your car.

Let's read that again: *Both INSIDE and outside of your car.* Yes, YOU have been at least one of these idiots at one point or another.

Go on and cry, Snowflake. It's about to get real.

In order to hit all of the bases, this book is broken up into several chapters. First, we'll start with a general list of shitty drivers so you can get a jumpstart on the idiots you're most likely to encounter on a day to day basis. A special section will follow this one that specifically pertains to people (sorry, I mean ASSHOLES) who block up the left lane, and the *Def Poetry* that often results from being stuck behind them.

From there, we'll proceed to the idiots you are likely to encounter at construction sites and other merge points. You will also learn what the law actually says about merging, so you can get off your high horse FOREVER about people "cutting in line."

After we're done with merging, we'll segue into parking lots for the most inconsiderate pricks on the planet. Keep your keys out for this one.

Next, we'll talk about the truly special (read – "Short Bus") strains of morons that drive fast during snowy conditions.

Introduction

Yeah.

From there, we'll take a slight turn and talk about etiquette. We'll discuss how to use your horn more effectively. We'll even have a short lesson in Morse Code so you can really let that shit for brains cocksucker know exactly how you feel about his cutting you off. We'll compliment this with a quick lesson in sign language so you can, among other things, flip him off in ten different languages.

Pfffft.

And then, finally, we will discuss aggressive driving and road rage. Call this one the "Anti-Prison" chapter because it's designed to help you remain a part of society. No matter how much someone pisses you off, and no matter how validated these pages may make you feel, you are not allowed to shoot people. You're not even allowed to yell at them, can you believe that? Well, it's true. It's up to you to stay in control of your emotions and it's up to you to chill the fuck out when Grampa runs a stop sign and cuts you off.

Repeat after me: "It's up to me *not* to shoot the idiots."

It's up to me NOT to shoot the idiots.

Good.

On this note, I'll say this: If you're the type of person who frequently *Goes Back to High School* to *Settle Things Like Children*...

If you have a million guns,

Or a collection of "tactical" knives tucked underneath your Dungeons and Dragons game pieces (Translation – You don't get laid enough),

Or if you ride around with a fucking brush guard attached to your monster truck that will never, ever see off road, and you think this book somehow makes it ok to lose your shit and hurt some people?

Please put this book down right now and pick up Mary Fucking Poppins. We're here to laugh, not spoil the party, dig?

All-Around Shitty Drivers

I feel that it is probably best to begin our journey with some definitions. What follows are the most common idiots you are likely to encounter on the road.

Ain't no Virgin – You're going down the road and you notice that the car in front of you has a wrecked bumper. You think to yourself, "That one's been *Fucked in the Ass* before. Sure ain't no virgin!"

Aggressive Driving – Operating your motor vehicle beyond its own mechanical limits and/or beyond the limits imposed by traffic laws. Examples of Aggressive Driving include:

1. Breaking the speed limit
2. Sudden and unsignaled lane changes
3. Tailgating
4. Swerving in and out of traffic in an attempt to "get there first."
5. Revving the engine at a traffic light in an attempt to bait other cars into racing, or bully them into letting you in front of them.

These aren't the only examples of Aggressive Driving, but you get the idea. If you're driving aggressively, you're basically treating the road as your own private NASCAR track, minus the fire-retardant suit,

Chapter 1

helmet, roll cage, and ambulance on standby. In other words, you are a great big, gigantic *D I C K*.

Ammo – Items that *Mademoiselle* gives her *Bundles of Joy* that will often wind up getting thrown at you while you drive the car. These items will often include toys, electronics, and food items. It's especially joyful when she gives them liquids, and then later complains that the car is a mess. Swell.

April Tool – That douche that decides to put his convertible top down at a traffic light and then doesn't go when the light turns green. Makes me pray for a freak hailstorm.

Asshole – Generic term for someone whose driving inconveniences you.

Attempted Rape – Driving so damn close to someone's bumper that it's beyond tailgating. It's fucking reverse towing, Asshole! GET OFFA MY ASS!

Backseat Drivers – Assholes who are too lazy (or incompetent) to do the driving themselves, yet constantly instruct the actual driver as to how to drive. See *STFU* for how to deal with these assholes.

Bad Breath – When the vehicle in front of you either burns diesel fuel or needs a valve job and their exhaust smells like burnt oil. Don't even bother hitting the "recirc" button on your dashboard, because it's too late. You have to get out of their *Jetwash* and roll down your windows to get the smell of that crap out of your car.

Bad Driver – The exact opposite of a *Good Driver*. Their driving behavior is usually based completely on emotional indulgence, rather than competence, respect, and patience. They often overestimate their own abilities, as well as that of the vehicle they are unfortunately allowed to drive on open roads. The proof of this is evident by how often they *Fuck Shit Up*. The *Bad Driver* may look cool in the movies, but in real life more resembles the anti-hero in an after school special. If there were no *Bad Drivers*, then .1% of the US population would not die every year in traffic accidents. If there were no *Bad Drivers*, there would be no need for this book.

Bad Negotiator – It's morning traffic. Not stop and go, but bumper to bumper and everyone's trying to make all of the lights before they can get to the highway. The right lane is going to end two lights up, which shouldn't be a problem for you because you are planning to make a right at the next light. Before you can get to the intersection, you are stuck behind someone who is stopped in the middle of the goddam lane with their left turn signal on. They don't even look for a gap between the cars to pull into. Instead, they are *Begging for Change* in order to merge. Meanwhile, you can't get past them to make your right turn, and they don't even need to merge right now anyway because the damn lane doesn't end until the *next* light.

This person is a *Bad Negotiator* because they should find a gap and pull into it quickly so that

- a. the driver there has no chance to block them, and
- b. they don't block the traffic behind them.

Feel free to give them a *Two Second Blaat* and an *Italian Salute* when you're finally able to pass their dumb ass.

Bait – You're driving down the highway and almost no one is on it. You'd really like to go faster, but you just got a feeling that there may be a *Smoky* in one of those "Authorized Vehicles Only" turnarounds that they frequently sit in, just waiting for a guy like you to think he's gonna shave a few minutes off of his schedule. Suddenly, along comes a shiny bright sports car, in the *left lane*, going at least 20 over the speed limit. You think this guy is your salvation, and you decide to become a *Barnacle*. You let him get about an eighth of a mile ahead of you and stay in the right lane, but *match his speed*. Then, you watch him carefully. If he slows down suddenly, then he probably saw a cop.

Chapter 1

WARNING: This strategy could easily backfire if you don't slow down quickly enough, or don't leave enough distance between you and the bait. Cops may claim to write the ticket for the first one they see, but like anyone else, they like low-hanging fruit. If it's easier to pull you over than him for the same ticket, you'll be a *Body Double*.

Barnacle – Someone who tries to use a speeding car as *Bait*. If they follow too closely, they may instead become a *Body Double*. Also known as a *Leech*.

Begging for Change – You need to make a right turn, but the asshole in front of you is a *Bad Negotiator*. He's parked in the middle of your lane with his left turn signal on, hoping that someone will let him in. Get a job, motherfucker. And while you're at it, learn how to take what's yours.

Best Driver on the Road – Me, of course.

Big Ears – You're behind a *Douche* and can't get around him. He's not the first *Douche* you've been trapped behind, and is perhaps just another in a long line of *Douches* that will interrupt your schedule today. Aside from being *Douches*, though, the one thing they all have in common? Big. Fucking. Ears. Seriously. Whenever you're trapped behind a *Douche*, they look like fucking Dumbos. What could cause this condition, you might ask? My theory is that they hear so many horns in their life that they've developed goddam callouses on their ear lobes! Here's an idea, *Dumbo:* How about you start flapping your ears and fucking *fly* to work instead of taking up space in the left lane!

Blockade – Two drivers, side by side, going the same speed. Neither moves as you approach, and when you pull behind the one in the left, they still don't move. (Also called *"Bosom Buddies," "Girlfriends," "Sweethearts,"* and *"Hand Holders."*). If the two vehicles are tractor trailers, then this is referred to as a *Sausage Fest*.

All-Around Shitty Drivers

Big. Fucking. Ears.

Chapter 1

An example of a *Blow Job*.

Blow Job – Passing Pedestrians so quickly and so closely that the wind from your vehicle knocks them down. No, it's not the "other" blow job. Get your mind out of the gutter!

Bluff – To make a driver think you're going to do something that you aren't going to do. For example, it may be useful to get a *Front Follower* to think you want to get into the right lane. You signal to the right, so he goes right, but then you pass him on the left. This can also be used to make a cop who clocked you on the highway going a little too fast think you went in one direction when you went in another. Just stay in the left

All-Around Shitty Drivers

lane until he disappears in your rear view and then quickly exit as soon as you can.

NOTE: Bluffing law enforcement will most likely wind up with you in jail and/or paying heavy fines. Might be better to *Take the Zero*.

Bluff Scootch – You're driving along a street where you have right away to several intersections with stop signs. However, the people stopped at those stop signs act like they are going to pull out as you approach, making you tap your brakes and delaying you both. It is especially irritating when this happens at a 4-way stop (see *Dipshit Shuffle*)

Body Double – You're on a highway, going fast but preferably in the right lane. Someone has latched onto you as if you're *Bait*, but they're not doing it right. They're too close to you, and they are in the left lane. As you drive, keep an eye on the "Authorized Use Only" turnarounds. When you see that familiar shape of the cop car in the weeds (I mean, who *can't* see those reflective "To Protect And Serve" stickers), DO NOT HIT YOUR BRAKES. Instead, let your foot off the gas or even downshift. That way, the copper's radar will show your *Body Double*'s car as the one with the higher speed out there. And, since he's in the left lane, he looks more guilty (and should get a ticket since he shouldn't be in the damn left lane unless he's passing someone anyway). Be sure to wave at him as the cop pulls him over because whether he wanted to or not, he's done you a solid.

Bonne Pipe – *(French)* You're driving down the highway in your tractor trailer when you spy a convertible Porsche driving slowly and erratically in the left lane. As you pass, you see that the male driver has a blonde head bouncing up and down on his lap. You give him a thumbs up and yell, *"Bonne Pipe!"*

Bosum Buddies – Two drivers, side by side, going the same speed. Neither moves as you approach, and when you pull behind the one in the left, they still don't move. (Also called *"Blockade," "Girlfriends," "Sweethearts,"* and *"Hand Holders."*). If the two vehicles are tractor trailers, then this is referred to as a *Sausage Fest*.

Chapter 1

"Bon Pipe!"

Bragging Douche – Someone with signs all over their car that brag about their kid. "This car houses an honor roll student." "Proud parent of Glee Club Class President." While you're at it, how about you add, "Proud parent of a future 23-year-old virgin." Like I give a fuck?

Bridge Pussy – Someone who suffers from *Bridgeophobia*.

Bridgeophobia – The irrational fear that grips *Bridge Pussies* when they drive onto a bridge, causing them to slam on their brakes, veer in and out of their lane, and ultimately slow down to a speed that rivals pedestrian traffic. Very common in New York City.

All-Around Shitty Drivers

Bully – A driver who tries to intimidate other people on the road. Several instances of a *Bully* at work are

1. Any car that ignores or even swerves at or immediately in front of a bicycle. Just because in a collision they die and you don't does not mean you don't have to observe their right of way.

2. Any car that ignores or even swerves at or immediately in front of a motorcycle. Here's some news for you: That bike weighs upwards of 500 pounds and is made mostly of cast-iron and steel. You will hurt or kill the motorcyclist, but that doesn't mean you can't die from that bike going through your windshield and then through your face. Follow the right of way, asshole.

3. A tractor trailer that disregards the presence of smaller vehicles when making a lane change. For the most part, OTR (Over The Road) drivers are courteous, professional, and respectful. But when they aren't, it's very dangerous.

4. A tailgater who's driving a *Large Penis Illusion Creating Vehicle*. I ALWAYS slow down when confronted by a *Pitcher* wannabe. The way I see it, if I'm going to get *fucked in the ass*, it should happen at a lower rate of speed.

Bump – When you are behind someone in the left lane who is slow to get over, you quickly flash your brights at them. This is called a *Bump*.

Bundle of Joy – A child restrained in the back seat of your car. Named with sarcasm for their propensity to scream and yell and throw food at the driver, thus endangering the lives of everyone in the vehicle.

Butt Sniffer – Someone who drives in your blind spot. You slow down, so does he. You speed up, so does he. He just loves that blind spot. What's he doing back there? He's butt sniffing, that's what.

Chapter 1

C – Student – This jackass won't pull up all the way to the line at a red light and thus hasn't tripped the sensor that tells the lights to change. More than likely, in high school they were repeatedly told they needed to apply themselves if they hoped to get anywhere in life. Well, they didn't apply themselves and now neither of you are ever going to get anywhere in life. *See also Spacer and Waste of Space.*

Catcher – In a rear-end collision, the *Catcher* is the vehicle in front.

Centipede – Multiple "pitcher/catcher" collisions in a row, resulting from someone slamming on their brakes . . . and everyone else not leaving enough room to stop. See also *Gang Bang*.

Cloaking Device – Someone who is driving their car at night without their headlights on. See also *Invisible Man*.

A *Catcher* getting *Fucked In The Ass* by a *Pitcher*.

All-Around Shitty Drivers

Closet Catcher – Someone who slams on their brakes for no apparent reason, almost causing you to *Fuck them in the Ass*. See also *Dude who wants you to Slam Him in the Ass*.

Cock Block –

1. This is the guy who rides in the left lane, next to someone going the same speed in the right. You politely *Bump* him to signal your desire for him to get the fuck out of your way. But because this shit heel grew up in a trailer park where bright lights remind him of the childhood gang bang he received at the hands of the aliens who abducted him (the space kind), he flashes his brakes at you, gives you the middle finger, and keeps right on going the same speed as the slow prick next to him. The more obnoxious version of *Hand Holders*, he may even *Take a Piss* on you.

2. The guy who tries to be a *Merge Manager* on the on-ramp of a highway where the on-ramp starts out as two lanes but reduces into one. He tries to insert himself in the way well before the merge happens because ... well, because he's an asshole, that's why.

Compensating –

1. Driving a car that is unnecessarily large, overly loud, brightly colored beyond even the most flamboyant of tastes; adorned with ridiculous ornaments and "performance mods" such as fins, spoilers, and nitrous systems; and/or with more horsepower than anyone could ever possibly need on public roads; in order to make up for a lack of adequate packing in one's pants. This condition most often pertains to men behind the wheel, so let's study this metaphor a little more closely. A man is feeling depressed about his junk, so he visits the local showroom for a cure. Suddenly, his mood is transformed by the sight of a car that can

Chapter 1

Compensate for his feelings of inadequacy. It could be large, like a monster truck, or it may even *look* like a penis, like a "Corvette," or a "Viper." More than anything, he covets this penis. He salivates with anticipation as he waits for the salesman to retrieve the keys to the penis. After an eternity of shifting his weight between his short legs, repeatedly adjusting the brim of his *NASCAR* hat, and scratching his inadequate privates, he climbs *inside* the penis.

With a smile on his face, he takes a deep breath and relaxes. He has finally become the dick he's always wanted to be.

2. Driving like a complete asshole in order to feel powerful. Usually the result of feeling inadequate in the bedroom, or never having been given the opportunity to share his penis with a live human. See *Small Penis Syndrome*.

Creep – Similar to "Lurker." You're on the highway, cruising along in the right lane. Over five minutes or so, this guy slowly gains on you (creeps up on you, so to speak) in the left lane. Once he's next to you, he maintains the same speed as you for a bit. The theme for *Halloween* plays in your head as you try your hardest to ignore him. You don't want to look at him because you're afraid you'll see burnt skin and razors for fingernails. You wish he'd just pass, but no, he just hangs out for way too long a time. Finally, he starts to move ahead again and your fear of being the next BTK victim subsides... until the next *Creep* comes along.

Criminal Restraints – Child seats, whose main function is not to protect the kid in a crash, but rather to keep them from throwing baby crap at the driver.

Critic – You're a passenger in the car with someone constantly criticizing everyone else's driving. Examples of what he might say are: "Nice turn signal, MAN!" "Where did you learn to drive, GRANDMA!" "Who gave you a license, BLIND BOY!" He's in his little bubble and assumes

All-Around Shitty Drivers

nobody can hear him. Finally, you tell him he should write a book about bad drivers and he says, "I will...Someday..." See also *Mister Supremist*.

Crowd Surfing – In heavy traffic, weaving in and out of lanes trying to find the one that will get there first. Usually, you just wind up getting into an accident or pulled over for reckless driving.

Cutting In Line – That feeling you get when another car gets in front of you. You should shrug off this feeling, unless you're in the left lane and they passed you on the right. If that's the case, you should pull over to the side of the road, put a gun into your mouth, and end your life.

Daddy Issues – Someone pulls in front of you when they shouldn't (asshole move), and then stomps on the brakes because they need even more drama. They think you MIGHT tailgate them, so they holler before they're hurt.
Alt Definition: Describes a *fille* who will blow you while you're speeding down the highway in a convertible and doesn't stop when the truckers you pass blow their horns. This is the kind of girl you want to settle down with.

Def Poetry – The profanity that ensues from being stuck behind a slow left lane driver. See the chapter on *Left Lane Assholes* for examples.

Dick on a Stick – A bicyclist who drives like an asshole. In every US State, a bicyclist is required by law to obey all traffic signs, and most bicyclists do. But *Dicks On Sticks* will frequently be observed doing the following:

1. Running Traffic Lights.
2. Running Stop Signs.
3. Failing to Signal (yes, there are official hand signals in every state's DMV rule book).
4. Riding in the middle of the lane while failing to maintain the speed limit.

Chapter 1

A *Dick on a Stick*

All-Around Shitty Drivers

    a. Bicyclists are required to drive on the side of the road unless the conditions there are hazardous.

2. Driving on highways or other motorways that are clearly marked with a "No Bicycles Allowed" sign.

(Also known as *Douche on a Stick*)

Dick in a Box – A tractor trailer driver who drives like an asshole.

Dick on a Broomstick – A motorcyclist who drives like an asshole. See also *Organ Donor*.

Dick in a Jar – A minivan driver who drives like an asshole. This one's kind of redundant, now that I think about it. But he's named as such because his frustration at the world is probably a result of his wife ripping off his penis (aka, forcing him to drive an emasculating vehicle) and putting it in a jar.

Dick With Tits – A *mademoiselle* in a monster truck who drives like an asshole.

Dinosaur – A disabled tractor trailer on the side of the road.

Dipshit Shuffle – When two drivers from conjoining entry points into an intersection (for example, in a four entry intersection, it would be North and East, or South and East, or North and West or South and West) can't figure out who's supposed to go first. They are idiots, but trying to look smart. So one will go a few feet, and then the other will go a few feet, which scares the first one into stopping, which scares the second one into stopping, which makes the first one think it's ok to go, which makes the second one say fuck you it's my turn to go, which makes the first one stop again ... so on and so forth. The effect to an outsider looks like two cars doing some kind of retarded dance that you may have seen 40 years ago on a Saturday morning cartoon involving a coyote and dynamite. Usually, you see this behavior at 4-Way Stops, Merging Traffic, and Roundabouts, but most often, you'll see it in *Yuppy Motels*.

Chapter 1

Discounted Car – A car that was apparently sold at a discount because it lacks turn signals.

Division Challenged – A driver who, on an unpainted road, takes their half out of the middle.

Double Tap – Two small *Taps* of the horn. Polite, but a little more insistent since they probably didn't hear (or chose to ignore) the first *Tap*.

Douche – Your basic, everyday dickhead driver. He drives too slow in the left lane. He turns without signaling. He doesn't go when the light turns green. He stops in the middle of the goddam road to flirt with the nearest 12-going-on-16 year old cheerleader. Basically, he cares about no one except himself and hears so many horns in his everyday life that he's developed callouses on his ear lobes . . . Which is why he has *Big Ears*.

Douche on a Stick – See *Dick On A Stick*.

Drafting –

1. Getting right up the ass of a tractor trailer on the highway in order to have its air pull you along. Greenies like to say this saves gas. More likely, you will end up like a *Headless Douchebag*.
2. You're in stop and go traffic, probably because there has been a traffic fatality up ahead and everybody wants to stop and take a look. Your suspicions are confirmed when, in your rear view mirror, you see an ambulance coming. When it passes, you pull in behind it so that you can get through the traffic. Definitely a dickish and illegal move, though it will save you time if you can pull it off without getting pulled over.
3. Turning on your headlights and pulling into a funeral procession so you don't have to wait for them to pass. Very

All-Around Shitty Drivers

illegal. **WORD TO THE WISE:** Don't EVER do this when the procession is made up of motorcycle riders, especially ones wearing patches that brag about being one of the "1%." Trust me – This does NOT mean that they are rich. Stay the fuck away and wait your goddam turn.

Drive-By Baptism – When you drive through a puddle on the side of the road, right next to a group of unsuspecting pedestrians. Strictly an asshole move, though you get extra points if they're dressed in suits. Maximum points if they're wearing a tux or a wedding gown. (See also *Squirter*)

Driving Instructor – Someone who should have done a better job of teaching your dumb ass how to drive.

Drive-By Baptism

Chapter 1

Driving With His Penis – A term used to describe a guy who drives like a complete fucking asshole. He has no regard for others' safety, much less traffic laws. See *Dyke in a Box* for the female version.

Dude Who Wants to Ram You In the Ass – This dude drives about an inch away from your bumper. You don't move, so he switches lanes and drives up *that guy's* ass. Basically, you and the other driver are being gang banged by this asshole and the fucking will never stop until you shoot him. In self-defense. (I'll be your witness). (See also *Pitcher* and *Road Rapist*).

Dude Who Wants You to Slam Him in the Ass – You're driving down a country road, going about 60. A dude pulls up to a stop sign perpendicular to you, up the road. He stops and waits for a few seconds, and it looks like he's not going to pull out in front of you ... But then at the last possible fucking moment, he does, and he takes his sweet-ass time about it, too. You slam on your brakes, jerk the wheel, whatever it takes to not ram your car straight up his ass. Then, no wave, no sorry, nothing.

What you need to recognize here is that while you are fuming about his seemingly "reckless" behavior (and lack of consideration afterwards), what's really happened is that his hope for getting you to engage in mechanical man-love with him has been foiled. You can expect many sudden stops along the road, so I'd keep my distance if I were you.

Note: See also "Mating Call," "Catcher."

Dyke in a Box – See *Driving with His Penis*, except it's a woman behind the wheel.

Evasive Action – You are on the highway, going a little faster than you should be. A cop passes you from the other side of the highway. You look in your rearview mirror for signs of his turning around to come and get you. The right play would be to *Bluff* him by pulling into the left lane, thus making him think you're staying on the road. Then, once you are obstructed from his view, you decide that you need gas and get over and off of the highway completely.

All-Around Shitty Drivers

Fawkery – A noun that described people fucking up.

Femme – A polite term for a woman who can't drive for shit. *Pro Tip*: If you must say anything negative about a woman, you should always say it in French.

Femme De Mystère – A woman who never uses her turn signals. Also see *Man of Mystery*.

Fossil – A disabled car on the side of the road. If it is a tractor-trailer, it's called a *Dinosaur*.

Four Way Dipshit (FWD) – There is something really wrong with our Driver's Education Classes when 2 out of 3 drivers have no fucking clue what they're supposed to do when they reach a 4-way stop. They sit there and wave at each other, back and forth, back and forth, like a 4th Generation-VHS copy of *The Karate Kid,* and then they almost get into an accident because one driver finally goes, and then the other guy gets pissed off that his "turn" is being taken away (true or not he does not know but fuck you he's him and you're not) and guns the gas. SCREECH! HALT! CURSES! And then they do the *Dipshit Shuffle* until one of them gets pissed enough to not give a fuck and turns into a *Suicide Bomber*.
    Crash! Boom! Insurance Raise! Road Rage! Jail Time!
    Here's how it works: When you reach the 4-way stop, you wait until the others who got there before you have already gone. If you get there at the same time as someone else, it's still not that complicated. I'll usually creep forward and see what they do. If they're an aggressive driver, they'll go and I stop and let them go. No biggie. If they're not, they'll probably be grateful that I got out of their way and didn't wave to them like Forest Gump on a shrimp boat. Jesus, people, it's not that hard to understand and you're not being polite by waving me forward. The most polite thing you can do is go on about your business so that everyone else can, too.

Chapter 1

Four Way Stop – A place where *Four Way Dipshits* gather to display their *Fawkery*.

Fox In The Hen House – You are on the highway and about a dozen cars up ahead is a *Blockade* or a *SausageFest*. Cars are lined up behind the *Asshole* in the left lane, but the right lane is clear. You, the *Fox* in this example, pull into the right lane and pass all of the other *Hens* in the left. You then pull in right behind the *Girlfriends* at the front. I fucking LOVE being the *Fox In The Hen House*.

Front Follower – This guy got into his car this morning with no specific destination in mind. He just started driving around, looking for a sign from God to show him where he should go. As he sees you confidently approach in his rear view mirror, he becomes filled with a sense of purpose. "It's the Messiah!" he yells. This is because you obviously know where you're going, and thus become a guiding light for this otherwise listless individual. "I don't know where that guy's going," he thinks to himself. "But it must be a good place. He's the Messiah, after all." You get into the left lane to pass him, but he gets in front of you. You get back into the right lane after a bit, but he heads you off there, too. This is similar to a *Golf Ball in a Garden Hose*, except that he's not trying to block your path. He just wants to get there first, wherever "there" is. TIP: Try to get rid of a Front Follower by *Throwing Him a Bone*.

Fucking Shit Up – Generic Term for getting into an accident. It doesn't matter who's fault it is. ALL participants in an accident are *Fucking Shit Up*.

Fucked in the Ass – When you stop suddenly and the guy behind you rear-ends you. See also *Pitcher* and *Catcher*.

Fuckhole Who Should Shoot Himself in the Mouth – Someone who stops at "Yield" signs and Roundabouts. (See also *Unyielding Fucktards*).

All-Around Shitty Drivers

Fuckhole Who Should Turn in his License and Take The Goddam Bus –

1. Someone who stops completely at a traffic light, even when they have a green arrow signaling them to keep going.
2. Someone who doesn't go right on red when the way is clear and they have every right to do so.

Note: This is one of the most hated of all of the drivers. If someone happens to call you a "Fuckhole Who Should Turn in his License and Take the Goddam Bus," then you should immediately turn in your license to the nearest DMV and start riding the bus. It's the law.

Fucking Boxface – You're at a red light, and the oncoming left lane is turning in front of you. Your light turns green, but the assholes just keep on coming. Even worse, because of heavy traffic, they can't clear the intersection and are now blocking you in from going forward. Now, you will miss your light. You stare daggers at him, but he just keeps staring ahead, hoping his embarrassment will end soon. Make the most of it. Lean on your horn, ease right up to his car, and then scream out your window, "Mind the fucking box, you fucking boxface!"

Fucking Europeans – People who do insane and crazy shit behind the wheel and yet somehow never get into accidents. They seem to either have a knack for predicting future events, or ghost-like superpowers that allow them to pass through metal unscathed. Best to avoid them. A good example of a whole lot of *Fucking Europeans* gathered in one place would be the physics-defying clusterfuck circus that is the *Arc de Triomphe* in Paris.

    SPOILER ALERT: It's hundreds of *Fucking Europeans* flying in and out of this giant asphalt circle with NO FUCKING LANES . . . and yet nobody ever wrecks. Well, except for the American tourists who instantly become *Roundabout Idiots* upon entry and promptly get *Fucked in the Ass* by a horn riding matchbox car driven by a 70lb native sporting a dirty Sanchez mustache and beret. Ironically, after getting *Fucked in the*

Chapter 1

Ass, these Americans often yell, in complete and unbridled frustration, "LEARN HOW TO DRIVE, YOU FUCKING EUROPEANS!!!"

Fucking Imbecile – Generic term used to describe someone who drives more aggressive than their abilities will allow them to do safely. Most often encountered during snowstorms or heavy rains or on gravel or unpaved roads. Too much about their driving "skills" are the result of learning from video games that defy the laws of physics, and rely on luck, rather than any real skill to avoid collisions.

Fucking Useless Should-Stick-His-Head-In-A-Civil-War-Cannon-And-Light-The-Fuse Cocksucker – (See also *Fucking Useless Future Murder Victims*). That asshole that STOPS his car on an interstate on-ramp, rather than merging into traffic like a normal human being. Rumor has it that Mikhail Kalashnikov was inspired to invent the AK-47 assault rifle specifically for these *Fucking Useless Future Murder Victims*. They may also have inspired Lancelot de Mole's invention of the Tank. If I could have an audience with one of these assholes (especially the ones that stop at the BEGINNING of the on-ramp to make sure nobody can get around them while they're busy fucking up the world), my speech would go something like this: "It's like how what the coach told you in high school. Get IN there, Son! YOU HAVE THE RIGHT OF WAY!!!" *Note:* If you actually own a Kalashnikov, you are NOT allowed to shoot people with it, nor are you allowed to run them over with a tank.

Gang Bang – Multiple "pitcher/catcher" collisions in a row, resulting from someone slamming on their brakes . . . and everyone else not leaving enough room to stop. See also *Centipede* and *Millipede*.

Girlfriends – Two drivers, side by side, going the same speed. Neither moves as you approach, and when you pull behind the one in the left, they still don't move. (Also called *"Bosom Buddies," "Sweethearts,"* and *"Hand Holders."*). If the two vehicles in question are tractor trailers, then this is referred to as a *Sausage Fest*.

All-Around Shitty Drivers

Girlfriends / Hand Holders / Bosum Buddies / Sweethearts / Assholes

Giving Space – Keeping a safe, or at least respectable, distance between yourself and the car in front of you. In ideal conditions, this space should be equal to one car length per 10mph of speed and should not change no matter how heavy the traffic is.

Golf Ball in a Garden Hose – You're driving down the road, going *almost* a comfortable speed. You'd set your cruise control, but the guy in front of you doesn't feel comfortable going at your comfortable speed. You get into the other lane to go around him, but he gets into that lane, too. You change lanes again and so does he. Eventually, it's like a game to him. You can either shoot him, or set your cruise control a few miles less than optimal until he goes away. His behavior is similar to *Front Follower*, except this guy is more of a dick.

Good Negotiator. Similar to *Fucking Europeans*, but not as crazy. We've all seen that driver who darts in and out of traffic. We love to root against them, since they seem to be *Cutting In Line*. Good for us, most of the time, this doesn't work out well for them. But every now and again, you see someone's aggressive driving pay off. In heavy traffic, they always seem to be in the fastest lane. They always manage to merge in front of the tractor-trailers, and they seem to navigate through traffic almost as if the other people weren't there. And in the end, they do get there first. Also known as a *Trump*.

Generic Run of the Mill Asshole – It's a two lane highway and he's in the left lane with no one on the right. In 'Merica, you drive on the right side of the road, and you drive in the right-most lane if possible. Even if you can successfully be passed on the right, you are still a fucking asshole if you drive in the left lane because you're forcing people to pass through your biggest blind spot in order to get around your slow ass. Get the fuck over, Asshole!

Give Them A Squirt – Someone is tailgating you on the highway and you're not the "tap your brakes" type of person. Time to wash your windshield!

Seriously, if you're at highway speed and someone is too close to you, washing your windshield will be like taking a piss on their car, and will usually get them to back the fuck off. **NOTE:** If you drive a real piece of shit car that you don't care about, or it belongs to your roommate, you may want to maximize the effect by taking an actual piss into the windshield wiper reservoir before hitting the road. See also *Taking a Piss* and *Marking Your Territory*.

As a side note, my windshield is the cleanest in seven counties.

All-Around Shitty Drivers

Good Drivers –

1. People who demonstrate patience, respect, and competence at all times behind the wheel. They observe the speed limit, but let people pass them. They are careful, but keep traffic flowing. They avoid driving in weather, and they never drive intoxicated. Most importantly, they get out of my way. In short, they rarely, if ever, *Fuck Shit Up*, and are to be admired and emulated.

2. Me. All other drivers are fucking morons.

Gravity – When you pass someone on the left, going maybe five or ten miles an hour faster than they are going in the right lane. If you both are using cruise control, the laws of physics say that you should keep going past them, but instead they kind of linger there. This is a sheep's desire to conform. Just chill and keep your cruise control set. He'll back off after he realizes that he's beyond his comfort zone.

Gridlock – When all traffic stops and no one can go anywhere. Usually the result of a minivan or a *Prius* driver *Cockblocking* or *Fucking Shit Up*.

Guy Who Hits His Horn All the Time – Pretty self-explanatory. This guy rides his horn all day long. You slow down for an upcoming stop sign? Horn. You pull into the turning lane too slowly for his liking? Horn. Sometimes, this is a cultural thing. In Puerto Rico, or in the US Virgin Islands, it is common to hit your horn as you pass someone to make sure they know you're there, or to just say hi. But in general, most people shouldn't do this unless they have someone dying or giving birth in their back seat.

The Guy Who Hits His Horn a Second After the Light Turns Green – Don't be this guy. I mean, what the fuck, dude?

Head In The Clouds – Driving without paying attention to what you're doing.

Chapter 1

Headless Douche Bag

Headless Douchebag – When you are texting and driving on the highway and don't notice that that tractor trailer in your lane has stopped. Oops.

Hillbilly Hee-Haw – When someone does something completely stupid (and often extremely dangerous), in order to pass someone. The two most common locations of *Hillbilly Hee-Haw's* are:

1. The on/off ramp of a major highway. People who stop here are completely useless human beings, so I empathize. Unfortunately, it's more likely to be you, not them, who dies if you pull a *Hillbilly Hee-Haw* into traffic going highway speeds.

2. The emergency lane of a major highway. I can't tell you how many YouTube videos I've seen of people being so frustrating by jackasses in the left lane that they go into the emergency lane to pass them … and then wreck their cars. No one's worth that, man.

All-Around Shitty Drivers

Holding Hands – Driving next to someone on the highway, thus causing a *Blockade*. See also *Girlfriends*, *Sweethearts*, and *Bosom Buddies*.

Inner Idiot – That impish character inside all drivers just waiting to get out and *Fuck Shit Up*. *Good Drivers* are able to keep the *Inner Idiot* at bay. *Bad Drivers* succumb to their *Inner Idiot's* every whim. Pro Tip: You'll know that your *Inner Idiot* is getting the best of you when you start caring more about emotional indulgence than logic.

Invincible Womb – The irrational feeling of security one gets when they get behind the wheel of their car. "Nothing can hurt me because I am protected by supernatural forces like glass and crumple zones!" Yeah, that about sums it up.

Invisible Man – Someone driving at night without their headlights on.

Italian Salute – Giving someone the middle finger. I don't know why it's called this, and I've got nothing but love for Italians. But the term makes me laugh my ass off anyway.

Key Bait – Someone who drives like an asshole and then leaves their car unattended. Interesting Fact: Car paint scratches easily and keys are always with you so . . .
  NOTE: It is highly illegal, immoral, and dangerous to damage other automobiles. As Travolta said in *Pulp Fiction*, "You just don't fuck with another man's vehicle." Be prepared for a fight (or worse) if you decide to do this.

Jetwash – The smelly exhaust from a diesel or old-ass car in front of you.

Large Penis Illusion Creating Vehicle – Someone driving one of (but not limited to) the following:

1. A truck that has been "lifted" or "sized up" beyond an appropriate function. No, you don't need a 36" lift to go to the

Chapter 1

The Italian Salute

mall. No, you don't need two feet wide mud boggers to pick up 'Lil Bubba up from daycare, unless said daycare is in the middle of a fucking swamp, in which case you should buy a damn boat. And no, Jessica Lynn will not be impressed by your 10 feet off the ground gun rack any more than she'll be impressed by the slim four inches you really have in your banana-stuffed Wranglers. Pro Tip: Use a cucumber next time, Short Stack.

2. A tractor trailer that has one of those "Jaws of Death" stickers on the radiator grill. Am I really supposed to think that I'll be eaten by your Mack truck? Really? I always slow down when I see this close up in my rear view, especially when I'm approaching a hill. Back the fuck off, jack ass.

All-Around Shitty Drivers

Note: Femmes drive these vehicles, too, and are many times even more aggressive than their male counterparts. See *Penis Envy*.

Lazy Cocksucker – While there are perhaps many drivers in many situations who could be appropriately called a *Lazy Cocksucker*, this is that person who's driving along on the highway in the right lane and refuses to get into the COMPLETELY EMPTY left lane so that traffic can merge from the on-ramp. It's one thing if the roadway is packed, and everybody understands that. But if you can get over, then please. Pretty Please. With sugar on top. GET THE FUCK OVER!

Leech – Also known as *Barnacle*. Someone who tries to use a speeding car as *Bait*. If they follow too closely, they may instead become a *Body Double*.

Little Brother – You're driving along the highway with your cruise control set. You gradually pass someone ... and then he speeds up to go your speed. Changes lanes when you do. Slows down when you do. Speeds up again when you think it's time. Basically, he's your little brother when you were growing up, except now you're fully grown and it's just fucking sad. (See also "Mr. Me, Too.")

Logistically Challenged – When a driver displays a complete lack of intelligence by stopping and doing nothing (and thus making the problem worse), rather than figuring out and solving the problem.
Examples:

1. A driver, for whatever reason, winds up going the wrong way down a one-way street. Now, you're already an idiot if you find yourself in this situation. There are plenty of signs that mark one-way streets in the US and you really have no excuse. You deserve every horn, every ticket that you receive for this, and frankly, you're lucky to have not killed anyone in oncoming traffic. However, the *Logistically Challenged* idiot will take things a step further by STOPPING

Chapter 1

IN THE MIDDLE OF THE FUCKING ROAD AND STAYING THERE. He's a deer in the headlights, unable to pull to the side of the road and regroup. Unable to put the car in reverse (another idiot move, but at least he's going with the flow of traffic). Unable to process why all of these cars are now driving on the damn sidewalk to get by him and honking their horns and waving their fists and middle fingers.

2. A driver is going down the road, barely managing to avoid the other drivers and medians, etc. All of a sudden, a really loud siren noise permeates the cabin, startling him. "What the fuck is that?" he asks, full of confusion. Involuntarily, his foot leaves the gas pedal. Now, he is perplexed that the car is slowing down. The noise gets louder and louder and flashing lights fill his cabin until finally, too much sensory stimulation leads him to press on the brake. His car rolls to a stop and he just sits there, hoping the aliens (or whatever could be making such a horrible noise) will pass him over and abduct someone else. Finally, an ambulance rolls up beside him. Both of the driver's middle fingers are pointed at him out of the side window. As the ambulance passes, he sees that the back doors are open. Inside the ambulance, he sees the three EMT's and a corpse pointing *their* middle fingers at him. The noise fades with the ambulance and the *Logistically Challenged* finally calms down enough to depress the brake, slowly press down the gas pedal, and slowly roll home...

The Look – Someone just cut you off, which in rush hour is tantamount to sacrificing your firstborn child in the town square on Christmas Eve with the Baby Jesus watching. When you pass them, you just HAVE to give them *The Look* so they know that you think they're a fucking asshole.

All-Around Shitty Drivers

An Example of *The Look*.

Lurker – You're in the right lane and he's in your blind spot in the left lane. He hangs out there until you start to gain on a car in front of you. As soon as you want to get in the left lane, he speeds up . . . but just enough so that you can't. He then stays in front of you slower than you two were originally going.

Mademoiselle – The polite term for your wife when you are pissed off at her, or question her intelligence. Reminder: If you must say anything negative about a woman, especially the one you are married to, it is best to say it in French.

Chapter 1

Man of Mystery – A guy who never uses his turn signals, or who, wink wink, is driving a *Discount Car*. Also see *Femme De Mystère*.

Man-Splain – When a man shouts at another driver, or uses his horn to get their attention so he can flip them off, for no other reason than the driver of the other car is a woman. *Interesting Fact* – In a recent survey, 30% of women reported that they own guns[1], so you may want to keep your *Mansplaining* to yourself...

Note: Like men, women are not allowed to shoot people. Not even if they are *Mansplaining* something to you.

Marking Your Territory – Someone is tailgating you on the highway and you're not the "tap your brakes" type of person. Time to wash your windshield!

Seriously, if you're at highway speed and someone is too close to you, washing your windshield will be like taking a piss on their car, and will usually get them to back the fuck off. **NOTE:** If you drive a real piece of shit car that you don't care about, or it belongs to your roommate, you may want to maximize the effect by taking an actual piss into the windshield wiper reservoir before hitting the road. See also *Taking a Piss* and *Give them a squirt*.

Mating Call – You're driving down a country road, behind someone who's going slower than you would like. Unbeknownst to you, he is a *Catcher Wannabe* and he feels like you're teasing him. To put it bluntly, he wants you to stop the Foreplay and get down to business, so he SLAMS ON HIS BRAKES FOR NO FUCKING GOOD REASON. In his mind, the perfect place for your car is straight up his ass and if you don't watch him closely, you'll make his dreams come true, Sweety.

Me – The most important person on the road. Now get the fuck out of the way!

---

1   http://www.people-press.org/2013/03/12/section-3-gun-ownership-trends-and-demographics/

All-Around Shitty Drivers

Me, too – Properly pronounced really quickly in a loop, as in "Me too me too me too me too . . ." You're driving along the highway with your cruise control set. You gradually pass someone . . . and then he speeds up to go your speed. Changes lanes when you do. Slows down when you do. Speeds up again when you think it's time. Basically, he's wants to be **just like you** . . . (See also "Little Brother.")

Millipede – A *Centipede*, but with tractor trailers or other large vehicles.

Mister Supremist – A little harsher version of *Critic*, *Mister Supremist* keeps his windows rolled down and yells everything he says at the other drivers. Did I mention that he thinks he's a much better driver on the road than everybody else? *Mister Supremist* doesn't just not give a fuck if you hear him, he *wants* you to hear his forecast for your lineage's doom due to your promiscuous mother's procreating with farm animals (which he has obviously deduced from your inability to execute a proper left turn). Though *Mister Supremist* has written some of humanity's greatest def poetry behind the wheel, it unfortunately has mostly fallen on deaf ears. Thank you, *Mister Supremist* for over indulging in your emotions and bestowing your wisdom on us. We will try to do better so that we may please you!

Mister What's Your Problem – This person drives in the middle of the goddam street until he reaches oncoming traffic. Does he pull to his side so both can go? Hell no! He stops and gives you *The Look*. You hit your horn to point out the obvious fact that neither of you can go anywhere until he gets his head out of his ass, but all he does is continue to stare at you with that dumb ass look on his face that says, "What's your problem?"

Mister Oh Yeah – This guy is driving in the left lane and suddenly realizes he has to get off at the exit that is 200 feet away. Does he shrug his shoulders, say to himself, "Pay attention, Douchebag," and make a U-Turn at the next exit? Hell no! Instead, he shrugs his shoulder, says to himself, "Oh yeah!" and then cuts across three lanes of traffic. All while not giving a fuck about the thunderous squeal of brakes and car horns from the people trying to avoid hitting his dumb ass at 70+ mph.

Mommy Issues – You're going down the highway. You pull into the left lane to pass someone and then they pull in front of you for no other reason than to drive slow and watch you in the rearview mirror while you completely lose your shit. To further add to the fury, the fucker starts *Flipping You Off*. Through said mirror you see that the driver is a barely pubescent male who probably started shaving last Saturday. Yeah, he's big and tough now, but once you follow him into the 7-11 parking lot ten miles down the road, put a gun in his mouth and make him say the Lord's prayer, all while he's shitting his pants and begging you for another chance to see his Mama just one last time... You realize that he just has some serious Mommy Issues and isn't worth the trouble.

Note: You are not allowed to put a gun in someone's mouth, no matter how badly or rudely they drive...

Motivation – You are driving down a highway and for a long time, with the cruise control set, and you see a guy in the left lane in your rear view mirror. He's kinda creeping up on you, but isn't quite a *Creep* in that he doesn't try to block your changing lanes. Up ahead, you're gaining on someone, so you signal and move into the left lane to pass. In that time, the guy has gained on you enough to be on your bumper. Now, it's time to do a little math. He wasn't going much faster than you before, so the odds of his going faster after you pull back into the right are slim. Therefore, he's likely to box you in if you need to pass again. However, staying in the left lane makes you an asshole, so what are you to do? Might I suggest you motivate the guy behind you to want to pass you. As you pass the fellow on the right, tap your "Set" button on your cruise control a couple of times so you slow down ever so slightly. Since he didn't see brake lights, he won't readily think you're slowing down on purpose. And since he will have to slow down a little bit, and since the lane pass is taking longer than his subconscious predicted, his natural reaction will be to get around you. As a final move, wait an extra second or two to get into the right lane after your finish passing, which will add to his impatience. If you do this right, you will have *motivated* the guy behind you to go a bit faster than you and the problem is solved.

Mr. Careful Motherfucker – This jackass is my arch-nemisis. Every five seconds he hits the damn brakes for no good reason. "Is that a tree on the side of the road?" *BRAKE!* "Oh my God, is that a car in the other lane that's about to pass us?" *BRAKE!* "Should I stop masturbating, and focus more on driving my car?" *BRAKE!!!*
    See also *Peu Manquer Rave*.

Mr. Farmer Motherfucker – You're on a country road with a speed limit of 55. In front of you is an ancient pickup truck, so rusted out that you can see through it to the glow of red coming off of the driver's neck. He's going a consistent 45-50 and it looks like he's hit top speed in what appears to be a 5th generation family heirloom. Finally, you reach a stretch of road with a dotted yellow line and nobody coming. You accelerate and move into the passing lane . . . and Mr. Farmer Motherfucker guns his gas with all that he's got. That ol' rusted box of bolts is kicking it, too. Usually that power is reserved for hauling cow shit and latrine juice, but today he's got an empty bed and is taking no prisoners because for you to get in front of him would be to speed up the impending shrinkage of his modest penis, which he is sure will happen if anyone gets where they're going before he does. Mr. Farmer Motherfucker is one of the most dangerous drivers on the road. It should be completely legal to torture, maim, and kill anyone who speeds up when you're passing them in a lane that oncoming traffic also uses, or at least considered self-defense to shoot at them to get them to slow down. Sadly, it isn't. One must rely on larger engines and modern mechanics to get around his inconsiderate and reckless driving ass. And don't bother calling the cops on him, either. Though technically what he's done is a crime (if he goes over the speed limit to block you), you were going way faster and besides, he probably played doctor with the county sheriff and his sister when they were all five and just as green as a junebug up on Pappy's Farm so many years ago in such a sweeter and better time . . . In other words, welcome

Chapter 1

to a modern-day reenactment of *Deliverance* with your playing Ned Beatty's role if you try to handle this in a civilized and law-abiding manner.

One final note: While Mr. Farmer Motherfuckers can be encountered literally anywhere in the country, I've noticed that they are particularly common in the south-midwestern states.

Mr. Me First – This is the guy who just has to pass everyone. He's not in a hurry, or trying to test the limits of his Camaro. He just wants to be first. As soon as he *is* first in line, he's probably going to slow down and become a *Cock Block*.

Musical Chairs – The game that *Sharks* play in a crowded parking lot as they try to claim the opening spots as the people finish shopping and reclaim their cars. *Campers* make this game particularly interesting for spectators, though infuriating for the *Sharks*.

One Second Blaat – Hitting the horn for a full one-second interval, usually in response to a *Wanderer*.

Organ Donors – A motorcyclist who drives like an asshole. Usually, they drive crotch rockets and do stupid things on public roads, including (but not limited to):

1. Driving at incredibly excessive speeds (30+ mph over the limit).
2. Tailgating.
3. Weaving in and out of lanes.
4. Driving between lanes (and cars) to pass, again at excessive speeds.
5. Doing *Stupid Pet Tricks*.
6. Racing other *Organ Donors*.
7. Flipping off or otherwise antagonizing the other law abiding drivers who haven't yet hallucinated that they are immortal and thus can drive however the fuck they want.

All-Around Shitty Drivers

A Future *Organ Donor*.

Organ Donors actually think their body armor will somehow save them from a 100mph impact with unyielding metal or concrete road barriers, or will somehow make skidding across asphalt at ridiculous speeds less injurious or painful. As my grandfather used to say, "There are two types of motorcyclists: Those who have been in accidents, and those who will be in accidents." But hey, the world can't have enough *Organ Donors*. See also *Road Kill*.

Out-Asshole – When someone is an asshole to you on the road (driving slow, cutting you off, etc), and you decide to be a BIGGER asshole to get

Chapter 1

them back (such as cutting them off and slamming on the brakes, showing a weapon, etc). Usually results in jail time or suicide by cop, so it's best to avoid this behavior.

Pacemaker – An old person behind the wheel. Named as such because they usually drive very slow ... And now, you do, too.

Peer Pressure – Paying attention to *Backseat Drivers*, which subsequently leads to making terrible driving decisions. The people who succumb to peer pressure are known as *Spineless Dipshits Who Need to Grow Up and Learn How to Think For Themselves*.

Penalty Box – When you're in the process of passing several people on a 4 lane highway and you pull to the right to let someone pass you, but instead they get right next to you and stay there. You can't go faster (because of the next car you were trying to pass), and you can't get into the left lane because of dickhead. You are trapped in the penalty box with someone in front of you and someone behind you. Then, you hear *Stealers Wheel's* "Stuck in the Middle With You" on the radio.

Penis Envy – When a *Femme* drives a *Large Penis Illusion Creating Vehicle*, or a race car, or some other inappropriate-for-daily-driving vehicle in an attempt to show that she is just as crazy and stupid as the male *Douchebags* that ordinarily drive these vehicles.

Peu Manquer Rave – Aw, what a sweetheart she is, dancing along to her Jay-Z as she cruises down the road. What's not so sweet is she's pretending her brake pedal is a goddam strobe kick drum and the strobe is creating a surreal rave scene behind her. Is she a *Catcher*? What the fuck is the matter with her? See also *Mr. Careful Motherfucker*.

Pitcher – In a rear-end collision, the *Pitcher* is the vehicle behind.

Point of No Return – The point on an exit ramp, or similar merge point, where you are committed to the turn and can't turn back.

All-Around Shitty Drivers

Prius – Used to be, people who drove minivans were the worst assholes on the road. Today, the Prius is the new minivan. When you're on a highway and traffic is congested to ten miles an hour below the speed limit, and then it eases up, that's usually because enough space opened up between the asshole Prius in the left lane and the normal slow driver in the right lane for the rest of us to pass him on the right (see "Pseudo-safer). Prius drivers are the biggest offenders of nearly all "asshole" moves described in this book. People who drive Priuses should be shot on sight, or at least given tickets for driving slow in the left lane.

Note: You are not allowed to shoot other drivers, even if they are driving a *Prius*.

Pseudo-safer – This is the asshole who is in the left lane next to someone in the right lane and who takes his sweet-ass time to move over... Except he doesn't move over. When he finally passes the guy in the right, he instead speeds up to faster than you wanted to go to begin with, resulting in your having to pass him on the right at reckless speeds... Or you could just remain behind him. Problem is, once he gets another car to the right of him again, he will slow the fuck down again. See also *Sumbitch*.

Puffer Douche – That guy who, usually in parking lots, drives in the middle of the goddam lane. When he encounters you, he does not pull to the right, as he lacks common sense. Instead, he just sits there and looks at you. He's like a puffer fish in that he's taking up as much space as possible in hopes that you will back up and find another way out of the parking lot.

What I like to do in these situations is pull right up to his bumper, shut off my car, and go inside as if nothing is wrong. Fuck him.

Note: This is a work of fiction. Your car will likely be vandalized and/or towed if you do this.

Reality Challenged – The perception that, because a nearby driver is in the left lane or driving a red car, they will get a ticket instead of you, even when you are engaging in the same illegal driving that they are.

Chapter 1

Repellent – A beggar at an intersection. If he's standing on the middle median and there are two lanes going left, for example, usually the shortest line will be the one closest to him (since the sight of him has repelled "decent folk." Get into that lane. And since he has made it easier for you to make the next light, maybe give him some change.

Return to High School – When a *Tough Guy* confronts you about your driving and you decide to get out of your car to *Settle Things Like Children*. The proper response to this is to drive around him and go about your business. If he happens to actually *Stalk* you or otherwise hang onto the past in a negative way, then call the cops.

Returning to High School / Settling Things Like Children

All-Around Shitty Drivers

Reverse Bait – When the *Bait* is behind you, in the left lane, and you are in the right. Basically, you think that because he's in the left lane and you are in the right, it'll appear as if he's the one going faster. But you only think that because you don't understand the laws of physics and how they apply to radar guns. Long story short, you'll both probably get tickets.

Riding on My Coattails – You're driving down a road with your cruise control set to 9 mph over the speed limit. Yes, you are deliberately speeding, but you read on the internet that cops won't pull you over unless you are going 10 mph over the speed limit. Though this flies in the face of common sense, not to mention the opinion of pretty much every cop I've ever talked to about this urban legend, since the internet validated what you want to believe, you're rolling with it.

You pass someone who seems to have their cruise control set for less than you. However, once you pass them, you notice that they *Creep* up on you, creating a *Blockade* in the process. What's happening here is that they, too, have spent some time on the internet and also found a site that validates their flawed beliefs, which is that a police officer will only pull over one speeder at a time. They are assuming that since you are "first" in the line of speeders, they can use you as *Bait* and avoid a ticket themselves.

In this situation, either everyone will get away with it, or both of you will get a ticket. Regardless, the people behind you will curse both of you since you are both *Stopping Up The Works*.

Road Hog – Someone driving heavy machinery down the road. Granted, in some areas (like in a construction zone, or in rural farmland) this simply can't be avoided. However, if you're driving a bulldozer, a hay bailer, a lawnmower, or a three or four wheeler down the road for miles and miles with a line of "normal" vehicles behind you, it's time to pull over and let them pass. You're in no hurry anyway.

Chapter 1

Road Kill – (See *Organ Donors*). A motorcyclist who drives like an asshole. Usually, they drive crotch rockets and do stupid things including (but not limited to) the following:

1. Driving at incredibly excessive speeds (30+ mph over the limit).
2. Tailgating
3. Weaving in and out of lanes.
4. Driving between lanes, again at excessive speeds.
5. Doing *Stupid Pet Tricks*.
6. Racing each other
7. Flipping off or otherwise antagonizing the other law abiding drivers who haven't yet realized that they are immortal and thus can drive however the fuck they want.

Road Kill actually think their body armor will somehow save them from a 100mph impact with unyielding metal or concrete road barriers, or will somehow make skidding across asphalt at ridiculous speeds less painful. As my grandfather used to say, "There are two types of motorcyclists: Those who have been in accidents, and those who will be in accidents." *Road Kill* are just accidents waiting to happen, and are named as such.

Road Rage –
Def 1. Failure to manage one's emotions while operating a motor vehicle. Can be as minor as yelling at or cursing other drivers, or as major as shooting at or running into them on purpose. The thing to remember here is that you aren't really angry because of the other drivers. You're angry about something else and using the other drivers as an excuse to exhibit bad behavior. Yes, sometimes people are assholes behind the wheel, but it's up to you to choose not to kill them.

Def 2. Losing your temper behind the wheel to the point of physical aggression. Examples of Road Rage can include:

1. Overuse of your horn.

All-Around Shitty Drivers

2. Screaming and yelling at other drivers.
3. Waving your fist and other obscene gestures.
4. Following (ie, Stalking) other drivers.
5. Throwing items from your car at other cars.
6. Attempting to crash into "bad drivers," or run them off the road.
7. Getting out of your car and confronting other drivers to "talk about" their driving like "men."
8. Waving a gun at, or actually shooting at, other drivers.
9. Anything that causes fear or possible injury to another human being that isn't in response to *imminent harm to innocent human life*.

(See the Chapter on *Road Rage* and *Aggressive Driving*)

Road Rapist – This dude drives about an inch away from your bumper ("up your ass," basically, hence the Deliverance-descended metaphor). You don't move, so he switches lanes and drives up *that guy's* ass. Basically, you and the other driver are being gang banged by this asshole and the fucking will never stop until you shoot him. In self-defense. (I'll be your witness). (See also *Pitcher* and *Dude Who Wants to Nail You In The Ass*).

Note: You are not allowed to shoot, or show your firearm to, Road Rapists.

Roundabout Idiots – At the time of this writing, roundabouts are fairly new in 'Merica. Truth be told, they weren't even covered in my Driver's Ed, which explains why I never heard of them, nor saw one with my own eyes until I went to Europe in my 20's. Therefore, I have a little empathy for older people who don't understand the concept of an intersection where NOBODY'S SUPPOSED TO STOP. But that's exactly what roundabouts were designed for. *NOT STOPPING*. The idea is that you enter into the right lane and people coming at you from the left pass you on the left. You then merge with that lane and *STAY THERE* until you reach your turning point and then you get over and turn. Simple. Beautiful. Very efficient, and not dangerous *UNLESS YOU FUCKING STOP!* Once you stop, no one else knows what the hell is wrong with you and everybody else crashes into each other! It's a clusterfuck of epic proportions and YOU are to blame! So do the rest of us a solid and *EDUCATE YOUR OLD ASS OUT OF IGNORANCE AND KEEP FUCKING GOING!!!*

Sausage Fest – Two tractor trailers side by side on an interstate, going the same exact speed, and thus *Stopping Up The Works*. See also *Blockade*.

Self-Righteous Douche – Someone who, after being called out (via the horn) for being a *Douche*, decides to expand on their level of douchedom by being a complete fucking dangerous asshole. You didn't like it when he didn't go when the light turned green? He'll sit there until it turns yellow and then burn rubber across the intersection. You didn't like it when he ran the red light going left in front of you and now you can't go? He'll give you the finger and throw an empty can of *Skoal* at your car.

Settle Things Like Children – To get into a fist fight over yours or someone else's driving habits. This behavior is usually exhibited by *Douches* who have been trying to *Return To High School* since the day they graduated (or were asked to stop coming).

Sharks – In a crowded parking lot, these are other cars circling and trying to get a space.

Shift – When one lane of traffic slows down dramatically more than the other. *Shifts* are welcome occurrences when dealing with *Blockades* and other left-lane drivers because they often open up room to pass.

Show Your Cards – The point at which you must convey your intentions to other drivers.

Example: You have someone riding your ass for whatever reason. Traffic is fairly congested, and you're in a sea of aggressive driving assholes. So you know that if you let this guy in front of you, he's just going to *Stop Up The Works*. So you play defense, staying with the flow of traffic, but keeping him behind you.

All-Around Shitty Drivers

Coming up ahead is your turn, two lanes going left. You aren't sure which one is going to be the shortest one yet, and you don't want the guy behind you to know where you're going, lest he be a *Front Follower*. Finally, you choose your lane, thus letting the guy behind you know what your intentions are.

Sloth – Someone who drives excruciatingly slow. At a light, they take a few seconds to let their foot off the brake. And then they idle through the intersection. The light turns yellow before they hit the other side and everyone behind them curses. The curious thing about sloths is that they seem to do this only when the people behind them have no option but to wait. When there is a way around a *Sloth*, they suddenly drive at normal speeds.

Slow Motherfucker – Pretty self-explanatory. It's a one-lane road and the guy in front of you is going slower than you'd like to go. In Ireland, they'd be courteous enough to pull to the side of the road and let you pass, but no, not here in 'Merica. In 'Merica, everybody's going places, and even slow motherfuckers can't be bothered to pull over and let you pass.

Slow Poke – A more polite name for a *Slow Motherfucker*.

Small Penis Syndrome – Driving like a complete asshole in order to feel powerful. Usually the result of feeling inadequate in the bedroom, or in life in general. See *Compensating*.

Smoky – A polite term for a traffic cop.

Speed Pig – An impolite term for a traffic cop.

Sore Fucking Loser – Someone who tries to stop you from merging in front of them, but fails. You get in front of them and they honk, wave their middle finger, cry, and finally pull on their pig tails. At the next traffic light, they get out of their car, spit their pacifier out, lie in the

Chapter 1

middle of the street, and kick their legs and pound their fists against the pavement in a dramatic cry for justice. In fact, they may actually say that.

"*Justice! I want justice for this grave insult to my family!*"

Chill the fuck out, dude. What the hell were you doing trying to stop me from getting over, anyway? YOU made the situation dangerous, not me, and you're lucky you didn't scratch my ride . . .

Spacer – That asshole who leaves a massive space in front of himself at a traffic light. I'm not talking about a little gap. I'm talking about ten or more feet of space – enough to fit another car in. Though he is probably reserving it for his imaginary friend, I always assume that he's saving that spot for me. Look, the guy is wasting space and causing people behind him to not make their lights. If he's first in line (see *Waste of Space*), then his light may not change for a long time because he won't trigger the motion sensor that tells the light to change. Running over his imaginary friend is the least I can do to let him know what an asshole he is. Five fingers to this guy. *See also C Student.*

Spacially Challenged – You're leaving a parking lot, trying to make a right turn onto a two lane road. The guy in front of you is trying to do this also. Though all of the oncoming traffic is in the left lane (thus leaving the right lane open), the guy doesn't go. He is instead waiting for the ENTIRE FUCKING ROAD TO CLEAR before he goes right.

Spineless Dipshits Who Need to Grow Up and Learn How to Think For Themselves – People who are susceptible to *Peer Pressure*. See *STFU* for how to avoid the temptation.

Squirter – When you're driving in a rain storm and hit a massive puddle near a group of pedestrians. (See also *Baptism*).

Stalker – Someone who gets so consumed with *Road Rage* that they follow a *Bad Driver* to their destination.

Note: Do NOT stalk people. You won't solve anything and could get arrested or shot.

All-Around Shitty Drivers

Stealing –

1. Pulling into the safe distance established between two cars on a highway. While some lane change is normal, this can be dangerous (and asshole-ish) in heavy traffic.
2. Taking a parking spot that isn't yours. "Isn't Yours" means someone else was stopped and waiting for it with their signal on. Definitely an asshole move.

Stupid Pet Tricks – Reckless behavior exhibited by motorcyclists on public roads in order to gain YouTube hits . . . or prove Darwin's theory. Just do a search for "Motorcycle tricks" on YouTube and you'll see plenty of Darwinism waiting to happen.

STFU – Stands for "SHUT THE FUCK UP." This is what you should say to *Backseat Drivers* who try to *Peer Pressure* you.

Stopping Up The Works – Two drivers in a *Blockade* that lasts a long-ass time. It's like they are playing a game where they earn points for getting people backed up behind them. Eventually, it doesn't matter if one of them gets over or not because there's enough residual traffic to keep the road congested for the remainder of the day.

Sucker – Someone who, at a merge point, lets in a driver who waited until the last minute to merge, even though that driver isn't actually getting over, but is effectively taking up space in two lanes.

Suicide Bomber – This fucking guy acts as if no one else is on the road, literally. Changes lanes without looking, cuts people off and doesn't even seem to notice. Hit your horn at him and he'll just cut off someone else. In his mind, he's got 72 virgins coming to him if he crashes, so why give a fuck?

Sumbitch – When you're behind someone in the left lane who is passing the cars in the right lane at a tediously slow pace. When there is finally

Chapter 1

room in the right lane, he gets over . . . but speeds up faster than you wanted to go in the first place. Then, when he catches up to more people in the right lane, he gets back into the left lane and slows down again. Sumbitch. Yeah, that about sums it up. See also *Pseudo Safer*.

Sweethearts – Two drivers, side by side, going the same speed. Neither moves as you approach, and when you pull behind the one in the left, they still don't move. (Also called *"Bosom Buddies," "Girlfriends,"* and *"Hand Holders."*). If the two vehicles are tractor trailers, then this is referred to as a *Sausage Fest*.

Symbiotic Relationship – The tender intimacy that evolves between two drivers that share a common (and often illegal) interest. One of you is speeding, and the other doesn't have the balls to speed that much and thus tries to use the speeder as *Bait* (like a *Barnacle*), but is really more of a *Body Double*. Both of you live in a fantasy world that the cop will catch the other and give them a ticket, when really, he'll probably pull you both over.

Tag team – You're on a winding country road, behind a *Slow Motherfucker*. This goes on for miles. Finally, the *Slow Motherfucker* puts his signal on. He slows down at an excruciating pace, but you take salvation in the sight of the open road ahead of him. You cannot WAIT to hit the gas and actually GET SOMEWHERE. He's almost at the intersection, just about to turn when . . . He stops in the middle of the road and waves to the guy at that intersection to pull out in front of you. Naturally, this new obstacle to your schedule is another *Slow Motherfucker*. You, my friend, have been tag teamed.

Tailgator – Someone who drives too close (up your ass), even when there's no heavy traffic. An intense version of a *Tailgator* is called a *Road Rapist*. If you hit your brakes and they actually run into you, he is called a *Pitcher* and you are a *Catcher*. Get it?

All-Around Shitty Drivers

Taking a Piss – Someone is tailgating you and you're not the "tap your brakes" type of person. Time to wash your windshield! Seriously, if you're at highway speed and someone is too close to you, washing your windshield will be like taking a piss on their car, and will usually get them to back the fuck off. **NOTE:** If you drive a real piece of shit car that you don't care about, or it belongs to your roommate, you may want to maximize the effect by taking an actual piss into the windshield wiper reservoir before hitting the road. See also "Marking Your Territory."

As a side note, my windshield is the cleanest in seven counties.

Taking a Piss

Chapter 1

Taking the Zero – You're speeding down the highway and pass a cop in a median break. You know right away he's going to come after you. You think about all of the horsepower your new ride has, how much of a head start you have on him, and so on. But you quickly come to your senses and decide to just *Take the Zero*. The ticket he's going to write you is nothing compared to the jail time you'll get for running away from him.

Tap – A small tap on the horn. The most polite way of hitting your horn.

Tap Twice – (see *Double Tap*)

Tattle Tale – That weirdo who, after you pass him, speeds up to pass you while filming you with his cell phone. All the while screaming, "I got you on video, Brah!" I mean, wtf, dude?

Taze – To drive slowly up to an unsuspecting pedestrian and then lean on your horn. If done right, they jump out of their skin, much as if they were tazed. This is usually done in parking lots and is strictly an asshole move.

Team Player – That rarest of drivers (especially in Virginia) who, when they see you approaching from behind, move over into the right lane. Sometimes, you don't even have to *Bump* them.

Terrorist – You're passing someone on the left, in a normal and safe way. All is going well until you see someone flying up on your ass in the rear view mirror. This guy is going 40-50 mph faster than you and doesn't look like he's going to stop. You tap your brake lights and he slows down just enough to stop three inches short of kissing your bumper. What a fucking asshole. If I'm in a good mood, I'll get over and let him pass, but most of the time, I'll assume the role of a *Cock Block*. Fuck that guy and his terrorist-wannabe ass. Maybe time to *Take a Piss* on him.

Three Way Tie – On a three lane highway, there are three drivers going the exact same speed right next to each other. This definition can be extended to a 4-Way Tie, 5-Way Tie, etc. In Los Angeles, I once saw a 6-Way tie and believe me, it wasn't pretty.

Throwing A Bone – This strategy is good for getting rid of *Front Followers* and *Tough Guys*. Pull into an exit lane and try to get him to follow you. Then, as he passes the *Point of No Return*, turn back onto the highway.

Tough Guy – This is the guy who didn't like you getting in front of him, passing him when he didn't want you to, or who is simply projecting his personal inferiority complex onto you. He gets out of his car to discuss your driving with you, as if he's the almighty bastion of hope in an otherwise crazy world, the Jesus Christ or Allah or Ghandi or Buddha or Jehovah or Bill Fucking Gates of motor vehicle operation. He swaggers as he walks towards you and his face may be hard to make out due to being eclipsed by the blinding red glow radiating from his neck. If he's armed, get the fuck out there and call the police. But if he's not, keep your window up or you may get tobacco juice on your shirt when he launches his tirade about Obama (he didn't care for him), Gay Rights (he's opposed to them), "them god-dam feminazi Trump protestors" (again, a vote against), and bad drivers like you. Whatever you do, don't get out of the car. Even if you "win" the fight, you're going to jail, where you will most likely encounter people who are a lot tougher than this jack ass. Don't be a *Tough Guy*. TIP: If the Tough Guy is postering at you while you two are at highway speeds, gesture towards the next exit, as if you wish to pull over and settle things like children. Then, *Throw Him A Bone*.

Trump – Two Definitions:
Def 1: *Good Negotiator*. We've all seen that driver who darts in and out of traffic. We love to root against them, since they seem to be *Cutting In Line*, and for most people, this doesn't work out well for them. But every now and again, you see someone's aggressive driving pay off. In heavy traffic, they always seem to be in the fastest lane. They always manage to merge in front of the tractor-trailers, and they seem to navigate through traffic almost as if the other people weren't there. And in the end, they do get there first.

Chapter 1

Def 2: The hierarchy of vehicles makes a big difference in negotiation. When considering a merge, consider also whether or not you'll get killed if the other car doesn't stop. For example, if you are in a Honda Civic, it may not be the best idea to cut off an 18-wheeler tractor trailer. Therefore, an 18-wheeler tractor trailer *Trumps* a Honda Civic. Just like any 3 or 4-wheeled vehicle *Trumps* a motorcycle. You're a bit of an asshole if you look at traffic this way, but this is a definition, not a moral opinion.

Two Knuckler – A person who stuffs their fingers up to the second knuckle up their noses at red lights because they think no one else can see them in their *Invincible Womb*.

Two Second Blaat – A two second horn honk. Usually reserved for people who have killed your children . . . or who don't go when the light turns green.

Two-Knuckler

All-Around Shitty Drivers

The Three Second Rule – In a situation that is not life-threatening, you should wait three seconds before hitting your horn. This is a rule of courtesy. DON'T be the *Guy Who Hits His Horn All the Time* or the *Guy Who Hits His Horn a Second After the Light Turns Green*. Give him a few seconds so that you are justified. Who knows? He may go and you won't have to hit the horn at all.

Two-Bagger – When you pass multiple people at the same time. Best I've seen is a 7-bagger, but don't quote me on it.
Note: In most states, you could get a reckless driving ticket for passing more than one car at a time.

Underachiever – You're in the right lane. A guy passes you and everything is going as it should. But then he gets over a little too soon and you have to slow down to avoid him hitting you. He drives slow now and all you can think is, "Why the fuck did you pass me if you wanted to go slower than I am to begin with?" This behavior often results in a game of *Vehicular Leap Frog*.

Unyielding Fucktards – People who treat yield signs like stop signs. Let me spell it out for you: If no one is coming, you DO NOT STOP AT A YIELD SIGN! A yield sign's purpose is to KEEP TRAFFIC FLOWING. If they wanted you to STOP, they would have hung a FUCKING STOP SIGN, you MORON!

Vehicular Leap Frog – Usually caused by an *Underachiever* pulling in front of you. Your cruise control is set to 70, they pass you and go 68 for whatever fucked up reason. So you pass them and go 70 again. Soon after, they decide that they want to go 71 ... but after they pass you, slow down to 68 again. No much you can do about this asshole. This could be a 1,000 year tradition in their country, or simply their *Mating Call*.

Vigilante – You are driving through a snooty neighborhood littered with mostly-unnecessary 4-way stops. You get behind someone who goes tediously slow, and stops for an excruciating five seconds for every

Chapter 1

single goddam one of those stops. They may or may not drive this way normally, but their main motivation today is to make sure that *you* don't speed or zip through the signs. The social tide of political correctness waxes and wanes for these people, as it does for real life vigilantes. But I've always considered them gaping assholes. Dude, if you want to enforce the law, go through the academy and get a badge and a gun. Otherwise, pull the fuck over if you love stopping so goddam much.

Vigilante Wannabe – You are driving through a snooty neighborhood littered with mostly-unnecessary 4-way stops. In the distance ahead of you, you see someone rolling through the stop signs as if they weren't even there. However, once you get behind this driver, they suddenly have a desire to stop completely at every single goddam one and take a ridiculous amount of time to get going again. They want to believe that they are doing this because "kids are playing" or whatever other nonsense, but the fact that they weren't doing this until you got behind them betrays their real intentions, which are to control someone else's life the same way their boss / wife / boyfriend controls theirs. Dude, get a fucking shrink, take a kickboxing class, get a new job, and GET THE HELL OUT OF MY WAY!

Wannabee – This guy appears to be a *Cock Block* when you first encounter him. Riding in the left lane, same speed as the guy in the right. But when you flash your brights, he's actually embarrassed by his own lack of vehicular political sense. He speeds up and goes into the right lane and the problem is solved . . . Wait a minute . . . He's speeding up. Soon, he's actually going faster than you wanted to go in the first place in order to show you that his car will, in fact, go faster. Hell, if he was going that speed to begin with, you never would have caught up with him and the whole situation would never have happened. Best to go ahead and speed up and get past him. Chances are, once you are a hundred yards or so ahead of him, he's going to let it go and drop down to his normal speed and you'll never hear from him again.

All-Around Shitty Drivers

Wanderer – (politely known as "distracted driver") – With 90% of their already limited brainpower on anything other than driving (texting, applying makeup, yelling at the damn kids, or just plain drunk or stoned), the car is wandering in and out of their lane. Typically, I'll lightly tap my horn twice as I pass not only to increase the chances of their seeing me, but to get them to prioritize the fact that they are *driving a fucking car* and need to *pay fucking attention*.

Waste of Space – a *Spacer* who is at the front of the line at a traffic light. The reason for this behavior is completely beyond me, in any situation, but at a traffic light it's particularly problematic. Most, if not all, of the traffic lights nowadays have motion sensors that key on the ten feet or so behind the white line. In fact, you can usually see the metal outlines in the pavement that mark the "hot area." And these assholes just want to sit there, oblivious to the fact that, for them, all traffic lights take ten minutes to change. If you want to wait in your car and do nothing, please pull over. The people that are behind you would like to get where they're going on time. *Also known as a C-Student.*

Yuppy Motel – Another name for shopping center parking lots. There's rarely a rhyme or reason to these things, and there are almost never any traffic signs. Intersections exist where they shouldn't, and medians are so prevalent that the entire thing becomes a *Yuppy Motel:* Yuppies check in, but they can't check out.

My advice for when you find yourself trapped in one of these fucking dingy and soulless places is to drive a lifted truck, so as to make your quest to draw a straight line (ie, drive over, rather than around, the medians) that much easier. Sometimes, the property owners will discourage this behavior by planting flowers, bushes, or even trees on the medians. The first two are no match for a decent Chevy, and neither is the third, so long as you get 'em while they're young.

Yuppy Playfight – When two *Tough Guys* decide to actually get physical and it doesn't work out as planned. Neither is Steven Seagall or Bruce Lee or Arnold Swarzenegger. Instead, they come off like bad Peter Sellers

Chapter 1

impersonators by slapping, lamely pushing, and even kicking at each other. Maybe one trips and falls and the other claims a knockout, then they argue over whether it was a knockout or not. The point is, they engage in just enough violence to get arrested, but not enough to wind up in the hospital for anything more than a strained back.

CASE STUDY

Let's go to the mall.

It isn't far. Maybe a mile of suburbia followed by a stretch on the beltway, followed by another mile or so of traffic leading into the parking lot. If there were no traffic, it would be a ten minute journey. Today, at 11am, we'll call it twenty.

Mademoiselle is in the shotgun seat, and your two *Bundles of Joy* are in the back seat, buckled into their booster seats like blanketed grapes. They're quiet, for now. But in spite of your asking *Mademoiselle* to not give them shit to play with, or snacks to eat in the car, you know she has anyway.

Mademoiselle is especially excited about this trip. Like a big game hunter, she slays the beast so that you can carry it. The long shopping list she carries is perhaps her not so subtle hint that you should work out more. But before any of that can happen, you must first get to the mall, through the sea of idiots in between.

The first idiot you encounter is a *Slow Poke*. He's going 15 in a 25.

Yes, it's 25 here, but this road is straight and wide and you could easily go 45... Ok, good he's continuing straight and we're making a right.

You get a block of freedom before you come upon a *Four Way Stop*. Of course, a *Four Way Dipshit* has gotten there first and now ISN'T. GOING. ANYWHERE. To the left and right of you, are other *Four Way Dipshits* who are all waving at each other to go. After a tense *Dipshit Shuffle*, your guy finally clears the intersection. Knowing the rules of a *Four Way Stop*, you aren't far behind.

Our next obstacle is a roundabout. Predictably, the *Four Way Dipshit* stops at the roundabout entrance, thus proving that he is also a *Fuckhole Who Should Shoot Himself in the Mouth*. A light tap on the horn prods him forward, but he didn't like that. No one tells *him* how to drive. He transforms into a *Self-Righteous Douche* and flashes his brakes at you.

Though the speed limit has now changed to 35, the guy is still going 25. You aren't tailgating him, but you are close to him because... well, he's driving ten miles under the speed limit. You're looking forward to the turn four or five blocks ahead (the one where hopefully your paths will change), when suddenly he slams on his brakes.

To avoid *Fucking Him In The Ass*, you slam on your brakes, too. The *Catcher-Wannabe* looks in his rear view mirror and you wave at him. You think you are making a gesture of goodwill, but in his country, waving means that you've just fucked his mother. He again slams on his brakes but this time gets out of his car to show you how much of a *Tough Guy* he is.

Feel like *Settling This Like Children*?

Rather than *Returning to High School*, you drive around the guy and are pleased to see that he drops the issue. Still, your adrenaline is pumping a bit and you keep replaying this incident over and over again in your head...

And you haven't even reached the beltway yet.

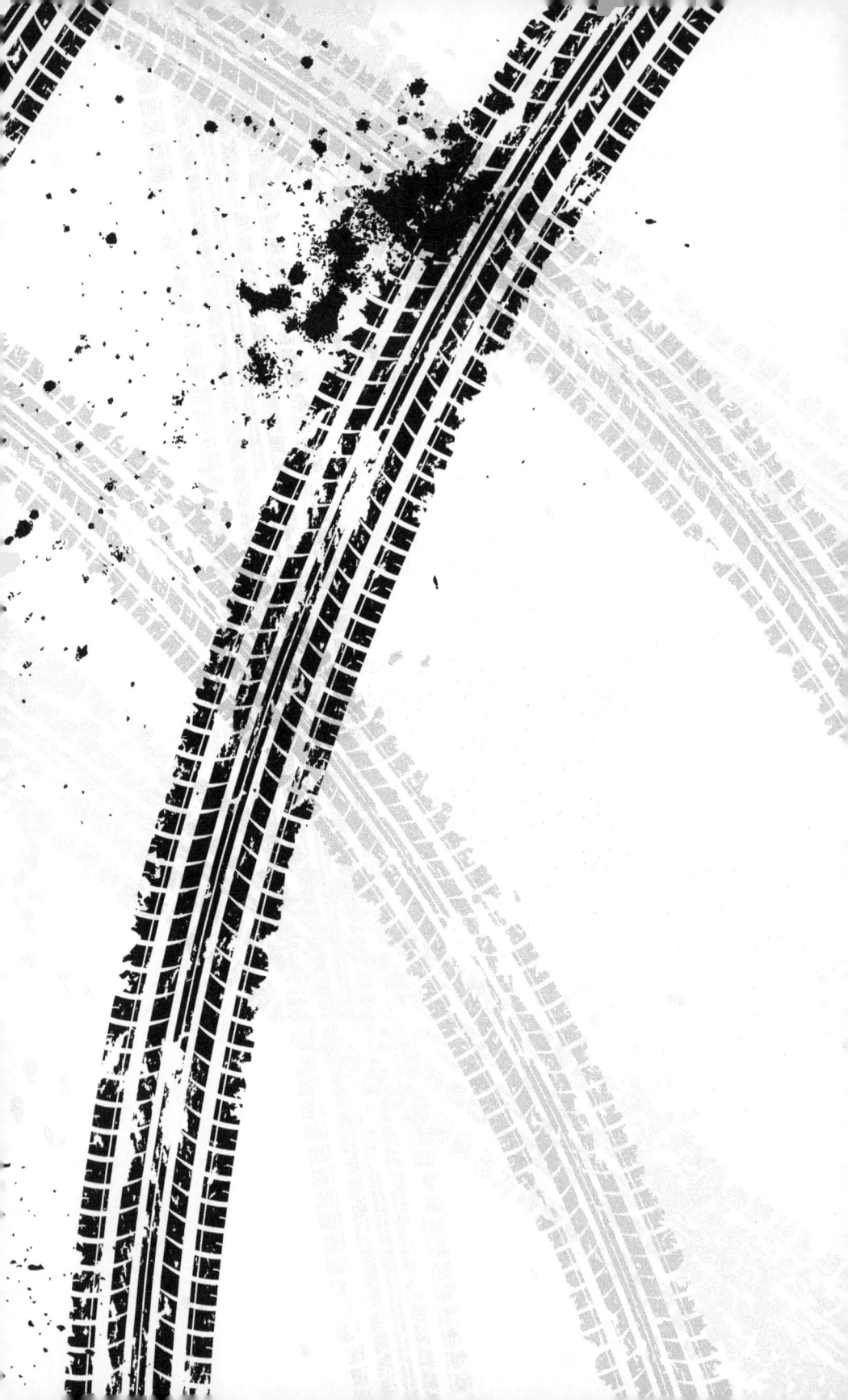

2

The Fucking Jack Asses Who Drive Slowly in the Left Lane

"In the Invincible Womb, selfishness abounds and hypocrisy is invisible."
—Ancient Proverb

"There is a special place in hell for left lane drivers."
—Anonymous.

"Fuck him. I'm me and he's not."
—Everyone who has ever lived (or driven a car).

CASE STUDY

Finally, you reach the on-ramp for the beltway.

You think that you are free, that it will be smooth sailing from here on out.

But you are wrong.

Not a hundred yards down the ramp, you almost become a *Pitcher* when a *Fucking Useless Should-Stick-His-Head-In-A-Civil-War-Cannon-And-Light-The-Fuse Cocksucker* slams on his brakes just before the merge. Now, you are really trapped. The traffic you're supposed

Chapter 2

to merge with is going 60+mph faster than you and the dickhead has stopped his car in the middle of the lane, and before the median ends, so you can't get around him.

He turns his signal on. You know, so someone on the beltway will stop to let him in.

Fuck.

Right about now, you also realize that some of the ammo *Mademoiselle* gave your *Bundles of Joy* was thrown forward when you slammed on your brakes. Specifically, you now have a leaking juice cup under the pedals. You put the car into park and reach down to get it, but it's stuck under the gas pedal. While you reach and work at it, you hear *Mademoiselle* say, "Honey?"

"Yeah," you grunt, still reaching.

"It's time to go."

You hear a horn, but the cup still isn't free yet.

Just a little harder and I'll get it...

A horn, and this time he's not letting up.

"Honey!"

"Almost...Got it..."

Distant profanity from the car behind you, joined in by more cars honking their horns.

"Everybody's honking at us!"

No shit, you think as you finally wedge the cup free. You sit up and the honking becomes more insistent, the shouting closer.

"He's coming after us!" *Mademoiselle* shrieks and you see him in your rear view mirror.

You gun the gas, but forget that you've put it in park, so you don't go anywhere. "You gonna move there, Buddy!" the jackass yells at you... But then again, you *are* the jackass, aren't you? You're the one stopped in the middle of an acceleration lane.

You've become the Fucking Useless Should-Stick-His-Head-In-A-Civil-War-Cannon-And-Light-The-Fuse Cocksucker...

You throw the car into Drive and wave at the guy who left his car. You easily pull into traffic and again think you are free. You're going fifty

The Fucking Jack Asses Who Drive Slowly in the Left Lane

now and you see brake lights ahead, so you pull into the left lane to pass them.

And, as fate would have it, you get stuck behind a *Prius* in the left lane in front of you...

* * *

By far, the most aggravating behavior reported on American roads today is driving in the left lane when you are not passing someone, and refusing to move into the right lane when someone would like to pass you. This behavior is universal, meaning it happens everywhere. And in the short time it has been tracked, this behavior seems to be on the rise.

And yet, even people who detest getting trapped behind a slow left lane driver will often do the exact same thing to other drivers.

Here are some interesting statistics that new research has shown in regards to driving in the left lane:

1. The resulting reactions of driving slowly in the left lane, such as braking and changing lanes, are responsible for over 10% of all motor vehicle accidents on highways.
2. Cars going 5 mph slower than the speed limit are more likely to cause accidents than cars going 5 mph faster.
3. Many of those driving slowly in the left lane feel that they have a "duty" to help slow down drivers who are speeding, an idea that even most law enforcement agencies disagree with (as they would disagree with any form of *Vigilantism*).
4. Many incidents of *Aggressive Driving* and *Road Rage* have been attributed to the frustration of being trapped behind a left lane driver.[2]

As of this writing, nearly every state has enacted some sort of "Keep Right" law. In some states, such as Georgia, for example, this problem got so bad that they passed a "Slowpoke" law with fines up to $1,000, plus

---

2 http://yellowhammernews.com/faithandculture/move-alabama-reasons-stay-left-lane/

Chapter 2

3 points on your license, which could cost you even more in increased insurance premiums. It was reported that in the first year of the "Slowpoke" law, over 300 traffic tickets were written, an increase of 50% to their normal "impeding the flow of traffic" traffic laws.[3]

As of this writing, there hasn't been a single study that has shown that driving slowly in the left lane is anything but unsafe. Therefore, no matter which state you are driving in, you should treat the left lane as a sort of "emergency lane." In other words, a lane you wouldn't drive in unless necessary to pass another car.

Having said that, some of the best underground poetic phrases have been conceived while stuck driving behind a *Prius* who's hogging up the left lane. It's usually a gradual process. You're driving along, minding your own business, and he slows you down.

You wait patiently, and he does not move.

You flash your lights and still he does not move.

Finally, there is enough room in the right lane for you to get around him... But then he speeds up.

You flash your lights again and this time, not only does he not move, but he gives you the finger.

And that's when the poetry starts.

What follows are some excerpts of poetry that I have witnessed firsthand in response to left lane drivers. Meant for amusement only, they may help you *Get Out of the Game* while you are waiting for the police to show up and write that douchebag a big fat ticket:

Shunt
Shart Cunt
Left Lane Larry
Leftist
Missile Targets
Jerk
Bastard
Putz

---

3   http://www.myajc.com/news/local/bill-torpy-large-few-drivers-rush-obey-slow poke-law/ZC09A35xFVdPV3ilvRYCAP/

The Fucking Jack Asses Who Drive Slowly in the Left Lane

Simpleton
Clod
Clown
Buffoon
Dildo
Dickbag
Dickhead
Fucktard
Futhermucker
Asshole
Cocksucker
Motherfucker
Fucking Dickwad
Penis-less Fuck
Motherless Fuck
Dumbass Fuck
Cousin Fucking Fuck
Child molesting Fuck
Deliverance Boy
Douche Nozzles
Herpes whore
Punk in a Clown Suit
"The pits of the American Driving Pool"
Pansy eating comatose victim!
Road hogging pig-shitter !
Brain Dead Worm Food Zombie!
Bullshit Greeny Douchebag
Diaper wearing Dick Smoking Cunt
Useless Fucking Creature from Hell
Cranberry Eating Vegetable Worshipping Penis Hole
Knuckle dragging, slow witted, moronic, idiotic, stupid left lane crawler
Shhhhhhhh ... Shhhhhhhhhit sucking cock-meiser!
Fucking Fuck Fucker ... *F-F-F-Fuuuuuuuuuuuuk!!!!!*
Stupid, ignorant, moronic, pathetically simple, inconsiderate,
    dangerous ASSHOLE!

Chapter 2

Fucking inbred, toe-sucking poo flinging monkey ball sucker!
Ignorant shitnuts jerkwad brainless spineless lowlife inconsiderate backwashing floorflushing scumheel lubestain dickless soulless twatbag!

Heard your own *Def Poetry* in this situation? Send your lines to jjmcmoon@gmail.com!

3

Merging Morons

CASE STUDY

Up ahead, traffic slows to a crawl, and then stops altogether. The *Prius*, which has been hogging the left lane for miles, puts on his blinker.

Most people put their blinker on in order to signal that they are actually attempting to get over, but a *Prius* driver is not "most people." Make no mistake: He didn't put on his blinker to get out of your way. He's doing it because he believes it is his divine right to get *in* the way of as many people as possible. He's signaling to reserve a space in the right lane while he *stays* in the left lane to keep you from getting around him. And, playing true to form, the minivan next to you slows down to open a space, thus boxing you in between them.

The minivan driver is a *Sucker*.

The Prius driver is an *ASSHOLE*.

A moment after realizing this, you also realize why traffic has backed up. Up ahead, the left lane is closed, which means that everyone that was in the left lane now must get into one of the two right lanes.

As time goes by, the space in front of the *Prius* widens, but he remains *Bosum Buddies* with the minivan next to you. After a while, you could easily pull up to the merge point (and so could he), but he doesn't. Instead, he takes up not only the space of two cars in two separate lanes, but all of the space in front of him as well.

He is not simply an *ASSHOLE*. He is also a *Merge Manager*.

Finally, you cannot take it any longer. The clouds above part, revealing a full moon and you feel a change in your bones. It isn't nighttime,

Chapter 3

and you aren't in a spooky forest, but you turn into a *Merge Maniac* anyway. You turn left and gun the gas, using the emergency lane to get around the prick.

Unfortunately for you and your family, he suddenly decides to accelerate as well and the two of you almost crash into each other. Seeing that he's successfully stopped you from "cutting in line," he gives you the finger...

You reach for the Magnum you normally keep under the seat, but it isn't there. Mademoiselle has moved it, predicting this exact situation.

Swallowing your pride, you realize that it was probably the right thing for her to do.

We've all been there, haven't we?

First, let's talk about how *not* to merge.

In our situation (three lanes merging into two), many drivers consider it polite (I've even heard "law abiding," which isn't true in any American State) to get into the right lane as soon as possible and then "wait their turn." In their view everyone else should do the same thing and leave the center and left lanes empty for *miles* in the spirit of not cutting in line.

I am not saying that drivers aren't welcome to do this, but I am saying that their logic, legal knowledge, and expectations of other drivers are severely flawed. Getting into the right lane and leaving the middle and left lane empty is not legally required. It doesn't make any sense to do this, as you're basically saying that people shouldn't be in the left or center lanes *ever*, and thus it's not what people are going to do. Once you get into the right lane, you're going to see many, many other drivers pulling in front of you, thus delaying your journey more than theirs. This will seem unfair to you and you will probably considering getting in their way or resisting their merge.

Which, of course, slows everybody down since the merge points are less forgiving than if you had opened up a safe gap for them to merge into.

Then there are others who will get into the left lane and go with it until they get to the merge point and then try to merge. Both the right and center lanes will indignantly cry out and call these people "assholes" and "dicks" and try to stop them from merging in... which is dangerous and in the end makes the entire merge process take longer than it should.

Here's a universal truth: EVERYONE slows down when one driver resists (ie, doesn't open up a safe gap) another driver's attempt to merge in front of them. Regardless of whether or not you think it is right for someone to wait until the very last minute to merge out of the closing lane, *THIS IS EXACTLY WHAT YOU'RE SUPPOSED TO DO*. In ALL 50 STATES, drivers are expected to use ALL lanes until they end and THEN merge. That way, more drivers can get through the merge point safely in a given amount of time. If you're in the right lane and you're seeing people getting in front of you that were behind you a few minutes ago, does it really matter? If you chose the longest line at a toll booth, you'd have no reason to get angry at the people who got through their lines first, would you? Same thing applies here. Next time, get into the shortest lane, and ride it out. It's not going to make much of a difference one way or the other since you are all barely moving. So chill, and stop it with the "I'm not letting him in" bullshit. All you're going to do is eat crow if he gets in anyway, or scratch up a couple of cars that your insurance company is going to have to fix, and then charge you for in future premium hikes.

I *ALWAYS* choose the lane that merges to stay in until the merge point, and it isn't because I want to "cut" the "line," it's because that lane is usually the most open. And why is it the most open?

Because most people don't know the rules, that's why.

Now that you do know the rules, let's define some terms:

Dotted White Line – Signifies the border between two lanes going in the same direction.

Emergency Lane – Often called "The Breakdown Lane." This is the part of the asphalt to the left and right of the *Solid White Lines* on a highway. It is reserved for *Emergency Vehicles* ONLY. *Non-Emergency Vehicles* are not allowed to use this asphalt unless their car breaks down or they are pulled over. If you DO use this lane to pass someone, then you are a *Merge Maniac*.

Emergency Vehicle – Often called an "Ambulance." A large van with flashing lights mounted on top, the word "EMERGENCY" painted on the side, and making a loud and high-pitched noise that is often called a siren. If your car doesn't fit this description, then you are driving a *Non-Emergency Vehicle* and need to get the fuck out of the *Emergency Lane*, you *Merge Maniac*.

Legal Asphalt – The asphalt you are legally allowed to drive on, which almost always is between the two *Solid White Lines* on a highway.

Non-Emergency Vehicle – Often called "Your Car," i.e., something *other* than a large van with flashing lights mounted on top, the word "EMERGENCY" painted on the side, and making a loud and high-pitched noise that is often called a siren.

Solid White Line – The line just to the left of the leftmost lane, and just to the right of the right lane on a highway. It signifies a border between the *Legal Asphalt* and *Emergency Lane*.

Suckers – These are the people who are in the right lane (the lane that's being merged into). I call them "suckers" for two reasons:

1. Because they have the mistaken belief that no one is supposed to get in front of them and
2. Because they often throw tantrums when people do, by hitting their horns or trying to close the gap in front of them.

I'll repeat: MERGE AT THE MERGING POINT, especially if you don't like people "cutting" in front of you. It's perfectly OK for you to choose the longest line here, just as it's perfectly OK for you to let everyone in front of you in the checkout line at the grocery store. But it doesn't make the rest of us wrong for choosing the shortest line, and when you honk your horn at us, or worse, *try to obstruct us*, you aren't just a *Sucker*, but also a **SORE FUCKING LOSER.**

Merge Managers – These are the assholes who both want their cakes and to eat them, too. They get into the center lane so that they can pass the *Suckers* in the right lane, but then they try to also block the left lane so that no one can get around them. The result is a complete clusterfuck that often results in *Merge Maniacs*, or even *Road Rage*. Again: **Merge at the MERGING POINT, not beforehand.**

Look, if you think you're an asshole for not waiting in the right lane with all of the other suckers, then you're an asshole, simple as that. Either get into the right lane and feel superior, or stay in the center lane and enjoy the fruits of asshole mediocrity . . . Or get into the left lane and merge if there's room, because we've already established that that's perfectly acceptable, too. But you're not going to cancel out your own assholery by being an even bigger asshole to other people. Most often, I will see this behavior by tractor trailer drivers, who for whatever reason think they are the goddam privileged elite of the highways. When this happens, I almost always do whatever it takes to get around them. Even though it won't save me any time, I want them to know that they failed to be a bigger asshole than I am. In fact, if they really piss me off, once I get in front of them, I may stop and wave at everyone else to go in front of me. You know, because I'm courteous and shit.

Just like they are.

In short, don't be a *Merge Manager*. Nobody appointed you "Cop of the Day."

Merge Maniacs –
Let's talk about "legal asphalt" for a moment.

For most of us, it is common sense what this means. It's the rock-like substance on which you are allowed to drive, right? Am I leaving anything out? Do I need to spell out that it's the space between the two white lines? That it's NOT the Emergency Lane nor the dirt to the right or left of it?

Chapter 3

As much as I'd like to use that empty Emergency Lane to completely circumvent the merge that everyone else is doing, I realize it's illegal for a good reason. There are some people, however, who don't see things this way. Not only do they feel that the Emergency Lane is a lane that's reserved just for them, they also seem to think that if they have 4-wheel drive, well hell, that median's going to god-damn waste, too, isn't it! You can almost hear their simple thoughts as they breeze by you in their monster trucks:

"Fire up the boy toys and make some noise! It's time to YEE-haw around this pack a lazies so I can get back to makin' sisters with my cousins! Mmm-MMMMM! Almost as good as making babies with my Momma!"

The closest I ever come to being a *Merge Maniac* is when some asshole designates themselves as a *Merge Manager* and the only way to get around them is to briefly enter the Emergency Lane. But try to keep in mind that you may be merging because of an accident up ahead and the **Emergency Lane** is for **Emergency Vehicles** only. It would really suck for everyone involved (including you, Asshole) to get into an accident with one of them. Also keep in mind that most accident sites, and construction sites, too, come to think of it, have police officers at them who would just LOVE to write a *Merge Maniac* a ticket. I believe the charge would be **Reckless Driving,** which in most states can result in heavy fines and even jail time.

Hmmmmm ... Maybe I shouldn't be a complete fucking dangerous dickhead after all, Earl! Cousin's just gonna hafta wait!

And Momma, too!

Merge Maniacs aren't limited only to construction / accident zones, and they don't always appear on the highway. Just the other day, someone used the acceleration lane of an exit to pass around me in the right lane because some jackass was driving next to me in the left lane and wouldn't get over. And I commonly see people use a right turn only lane as a way to get to the front of the line and then put their left turn signal on as if they had just realized their lane ends. Being passive-aggressive is still aggressive, and in most law books, aggressive driving is reckless driving (or worse). I totally understand your frustration, but if you think waiting for numnuts to get out of your way was tedious, try waiting for

Merging Morons

30 days to get out of jail with your virginity intact. Puts things into perspective, doesn't it?

Sore Fucking Loser – Someone who tries to stop you from merging in front of them, but fails. You get in front of them and they honk, wave their middle finger, cry, and finally pull on their pig tails. At the next traffic light, they get out of their car, spit their pacifier out, lie in the middle of the street, and kick their legs and pound their fists against the pavement in a dramatic cry for justice.

They may actually say that:

"*Justice! I want justice for this grave insult to my family!*"

Chill the fuck out, dude. We're legally required to merge, so what the hell were you doing trying to stop me from getting over, anyway? YOU made the situation dangerous, not me.

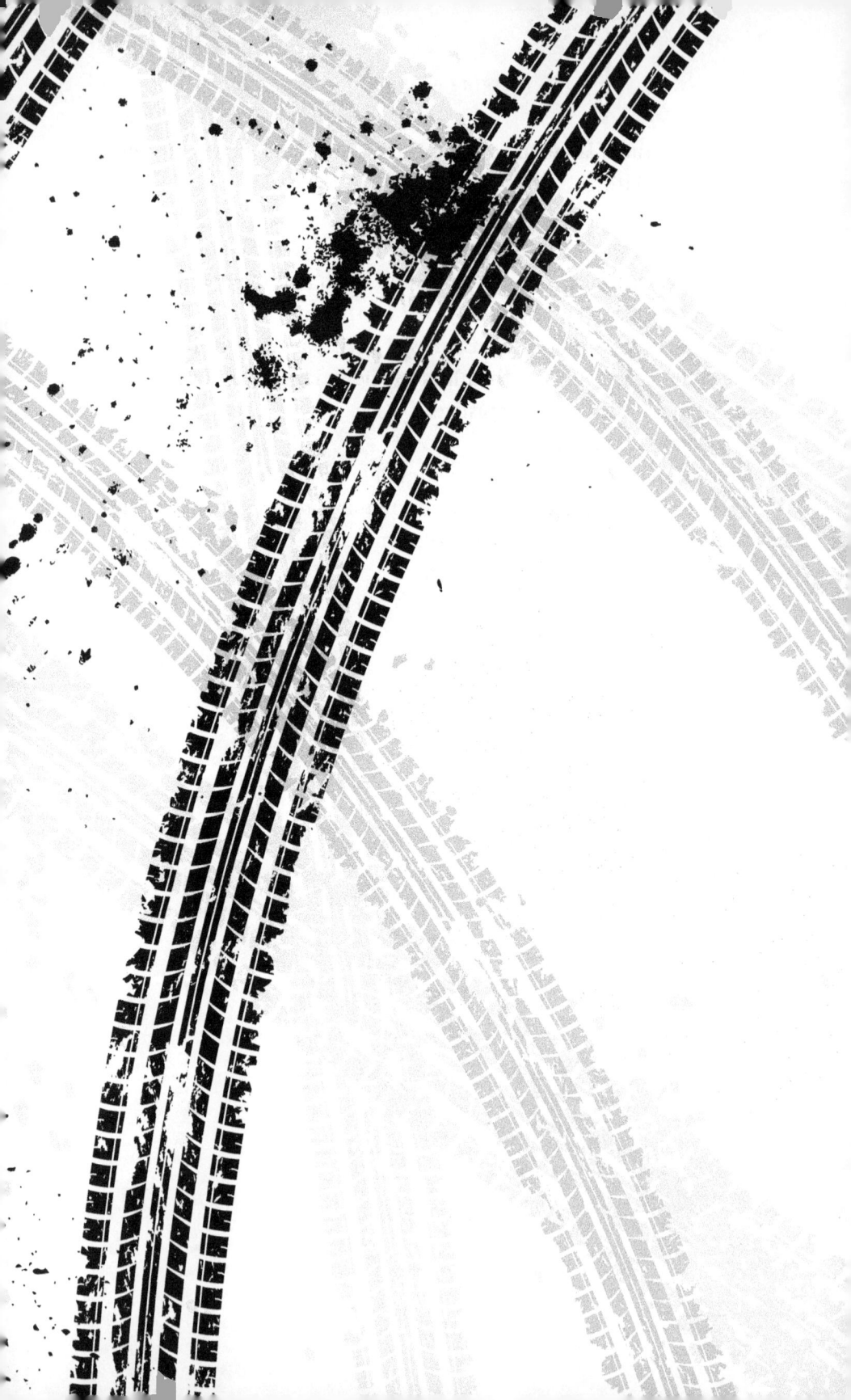

Toll Booth Idiots

CASE STUDY

Once you reach the end of the construction zone, traffic speeds up and you are finally able to get around the Prius. Not that he got over or anything. In fact, he sped up to stay in front of you. But with three lanes open and your SUV having a larger engine than his cute little green battery pack, you are able to pass him.

Unfortunately, your victory is short lived. Up ahead is a toll booth and you haven't charged your EZ Pass. Rather than risk a $150 ticket, you drive to the right, towards the "Cash" lane.

What follows are a variety of idiots that you are likely to encounter.

Bad Jester – A *Silly Trickster* who takes the joke too far and tries to talk the toll attendant into letting them go through for free. They won't.

Dickhead – That guy who cuts in front of others waiting in line at the toll booth. Really? Like you're going to get through the traffic any faster?

Doctor without Patience – Someone who goes into the "Full Service" line, but then leans on his horn because the line is moving too slowly.

Dukes of Hazard – Someone who goes through the toll booth too fast and winds up launching himself into or over the fucking thing.

Chapter 4

Dukes of Hazard

EZ Death Mines – People who are too dumb to read the sign that says, "EZ Pass Express ONLY," but somehow see the sign that says, "$500 fine for violators." The result is that they stop their fucking cars in the middle of the goddam highway and try to back up, into oncoming traffic, so as to avoid the fine. First, you're getting fined anyway because the detector has more range than you think. Secondly, you're probably going to get a reckless driving ticket and lose your license (as you should). And thirdly, you're probably going to kill somebody! Just *Take The Zero* and next time, READ THE GODDAM SIGNS BEFORE ZIPPING THROUGH TO THE EZ PASS LANE!!!

Head Shaker – Someone who pulls up to the "Exact Change" lane and honks because it won't accept dollar bills.

Idiot Who Should Have Swallowed His Tongue Long Ago – A *Head Shaker* who continues to sit in the "Exchange Change" line, honking his horn like a 2 year old on the potty who needs a wipe. He'll never stop, even if he can reverse out of the lane. And in spite of the rage that is quickly spreading through the drivers that are inconvenienced by this asshole, the toll booth "attendants" just think he's funny.

Toll Booth Idiots

Mr. Fuck This – Someone who decides that paying tolls is not for them and tries to crash their way through the toll gate.

Obstacle – Someone who, for whatever reason, winds up blocking a toll lane.

Mr. Fuck This

Oopsie – A generic term for an accident at a toll booth.

Silly Tricksters – Someone who throws pennies into the "Exact Change" basket and hopes the machine will let them through anyway. It won't.

Technologically Challenged – Someone who tries to scam the EZ Pass system (and you) by pulling up all the way to the gate and hoping that you will pull up enough for their toll to be on *your* bill. They obviously don't know how EZ Pass works, which in layman's terms, is quite easy. It's highly directional and three dimensional, which means that the machine will know you have pulled up to the gate without an EZ Pass. In the end, the *Technologically Challenged* has become an Obstacle.

Tongue Waggers – People who, in the "Cash" Lane, start up and maintain a long conversation with the toll booth attendant. They want to appear to be nice, but if that's what they really wanted, they would think about the long line of cars waiting behind them and GET OUT OF THE WAY.

Oopsie

Chapter 4

Ziggy Zaggies – People who compulsively go from lane to lane at toll booths in search of the quickest one. They almost never save time by doing this... Unless they are *Fucking Europeans*.

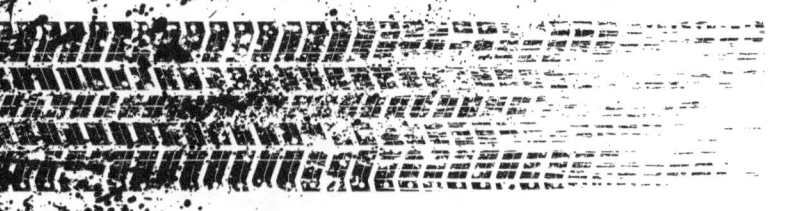

A Lesson in Parking Ettiquette

The absolute worst thing *Mademoiselle* could say to you (other than "I've seen bigger") is, "On the way to the mall, let's swing by WalMart for a few things." After everything you've just been through on this trip, you think about how much better it would be to visit a zombie parade. Or to be waked by a house fire.

Or be in the middle of a ferocious wet dream with a swimsuit model and then get waked up by your kids jumping on your nuts with BOTH knees while demanding pancakes.

Even *that* would be better than taking a family trip to fucking WalMart.

Going to WalMart sucks, but not because the store isn't awesome in its own way. Once you're inside WalMart, it's all good. Literally everything you need to prepare for an apocalypse can be bought there... which is good because said apocalypse is happening in the parking lot.

Here is where you get your zombie parade. Complete with extreme obesity, armored handicapped vehicles, and sometimes, like during a Black Friday sale, burning shells of cars.

I mean, what the fuck is wrong with people? Just about every single internet meme about human depravity seems to have been photographed either inside a WalMart or in the WalMart parking lot. Remember that movie, "Rainman," when Tom Cruise drills it into Dustin Hoffman's head that "K-Mart Sucks?" Perhaps it's time for a remake.

Chapter 5

A Black Friday sale at Wal-Mart

Anyway... After a short discussion with Mademoiselle (read – VERY short) consisting of your saying "Are you sure?" followed by a flogging of 40 lashes and a truckload and a half of guilt, you find the parking lot easily enough. With visions of a trunk full of sparkling and useless shit, you wait with tedious and mind-numbing anticipation for the light to change.

And when it finally does, you found yourself trapped in a *Yuppy Motel*.

"*Where yuppies check in, but they don't check out.*"

From the street, it looked like a wide open parking lot, but now you see that it's just a maze. In the real world, most streets actually go somewhere. But the rows in this parking lot end at medians. Even the ones that look like they are exits simply turn you around and guide you back to the fucking store. And to compound things further, the place is filled with self-righteous and indignant idiots who are all playing a combative game of *Musical Chairs* as they try to steal the spaces you've scoped out.

As egocentric as people are when they're driving out on an open road, it is truly amazing how much more egocentric, and dangerous, they get when they are shopping. Fucking assholes is the word for it. People are dicks in parking lots and few even realize it.

Let's start off with a few ground rules:

A Lesson in Parking Ettiquette

RULE #1 Your hazard lights do NOT give you license to engage in asshole activity. Ever park illegally in front of a parking attendant? Did turning on your hazards make him apologize and take back the ticket? Of course not. Hazards are meant to make your car easier to see in fog, or on the side of the road at night... And easier for parking attendants to target the most assholish of people in parking lots.

RULE #2 YIELD to pedestrians. I know they're called "Parking Lots," but really, the place is all about pedestrians. If you don't yield, especially in crosswalks, you are at a minimum, an asshole, and in most states, a criminal.

RULE #3 Park in designated spots. Yes, I know you're proud of your 4-wheel drive. Yes, I know no one is using those handicapped spots right now. Yes, I know the median is closer than the open spaces. Park in a designated spot anyway, Dickhead.

RULE #4 This isn't Nigeria. Parking your car is NOT a contact sport.

People completely lose their sense of social poise when they enter parking lots. Why is it not ok to butt in line when checking out of a store, but it is ok to try to run someone over in a crosswalk? The *Invincible Womb* makes people do stupid (and often dangerous) things on all roads, but in parking lots, there are many, many different species of assholes.

Definitions

Bully – Also known as a "Punk" or a "Piece of shit." When driving past the front of the store, this person guns the engine to intimidate the

Chapter 5

people trying to use the crosswalk. God forbid the *Bully* should have to stop for a few extra seconds to let a family of five go home without tire tracks on their faces. In most states, failing to yield at a pedestrian crosswalk is illegal, including those at shopping centers. In Richmond, VA, this became such a problem that many of these stores staff police to ticket *Bullies* who fail to yield... and a lot of other things.

Campers – You're in a busy parking lot, full of people busily circling the maze in search of an open spot, when you spy a couple walking away from the mall and towards their car. You watch them, hoping their car is near you and... YES! They get into a car RIGHT IN FRONT OF YOU! Great success! You stop and put on your blinker... And wait. And wait...

And wait some more...
What the hell are they doing in there? What is taking them so long?
Did she just now realize that she's ovulating and they have to make a baby *right now*?
Seriously – What the everloving fuck is going on?
Most people will leave this situation in frustration and find another space. But not me. I get out of my car, knock on their window, and then ask them politely if they are leaving. Usually, they will apologize and leave quickly, even if they are, in fact, mid-coitus. *Pro Tip:* If you want a faster result, and they *are* mid-coitus, start taking pictures of them with your phone. Or pull your dick out and masturbate. Just as effective.
Note: You can be arrested and labeled a sex offender for life if you masturbate in public.

Cholesterol – In a busy parking lot, these people turn off their car and wait for a spot to open. This wouldn't be a problem except that they are IN THE PARKING LOT LANES. This is even worse than parking your car on a public road because parking spaces require even more space to get out of. Now, everyone else has to drive around them. And if someone can't do this because they can't get around the obstacle (or are too dumb to), then this asshole has the same effect on this parking lot as cholesterol does on the heart. Gridlock... Heart attack... Death...

A Lesson in Parking Ettiquette

Conquestadores – *Entrepreneurs* who park on top of snow mountains made by snow plows in parking lots. Also known as "fucking jackasses." NOTE: This is in no way meant to reference people who speak Spanish, who, from a skills perspective, tend to be some of the best drivers on the road. I just thought *Conquestadores* sounded cool. Go on and say it. Cool, right?

Cows – People who try to back into a parking space, but have no idea how to do so and wind up taking three years to finish. They back up an inch, turn the wheel all the way in one direction, and then go forward an inch. This repeats over and over again until you just want to get out of your car and tell them that there's plenty of room on either side of them. But you don't, because you're polite and shit. Then, they see someone walking through the parking lot (or any other nonsense distraction), and they freeze, just like a big fucking cow in the middle of the world that no one can get around. I mean, come on, dude. If you don't know how to back into your parking space in a reasonable amount of time, maybe you should just pull in. Or better yet, take some driving lessons to get better at it!

Crossing Swords – When two people across the aisle from each other back out at the same time and crash into each other. *Pro Tip:* If you witness this happening, ask the one with a fancy car if he'd like to buy your testimony that it was all the other guy's fault. Good for a quick $50, at least.

Engineers – A *Yuppy Motel* is a frustrating place to be. Set up like a maze, it can be difficult to get in and out of without wasting a whole lot of time and raising your blood pressure. *Engineers* find their way around this problem by purchasing large "Off Road" vehicles and driving a straight line to their destination.
    Medians?
    No problem, I got 4-wheel drive AND monster tires!
    Bushes on the median?
    No problem, I got a brush guard, too!

Chapter 5

Trees on the median?

Not a problem, so long as I get 'em while they're young!

Personally, I think *Engineers* are awesome as their actions scream out a big "Fuck you" to the people who built the *Yuppy Motels*. Come to think of it, maybe I should get a monster truck...

Note: Engineers who don't actually vandalize the property are called "Free Thinkers."

Entrepreneurs – People who make their own parking spots. They will park on the sidewalk, off-road, and in the stripe-painted areas on the row edges. The truly awesome ones are *Conquestadores*.

Free Thinkers – People who drive across parking spaces that no one is using, to make a straight line to their destination. *Note: If they vandalize property or cross medians in doing this, they are called Engineers.*

Fucking Imbeciles – People who drive faster than 15 mph through a parking lot. Actually, 10mph is probably too fast. WTF?

Gluttons – People who take up multiple spaces in a parking lot.

1. **Lazy Glutton** – Someone who didn't take the time to pull in / back in properly and could give two shits because they're them and you're not.
2. **Douchebag Glutton** – Someone who purposefully takes up two spaces because they drive a fancy car. NOTE: This can be acceptable IF the spaces they take are on the outskirts of the parking lot. No one else wants those spaces anyway, so they're not hurting anybody. But if they're near the front, they are *Key Bait*.

Handicapped Wannabees – People who park in handicapped spots without a sticker, or for a damn good reason. Hey, I've been to the DMV and it sucks. If you're handicapped, this is a major fucking inconvenience, which is why society has chosen to reserve the best spots in the

A Lesson in Ettiquette

parking lot for handicapped people to begin with. So if you don't have a sticker but you walk with a serious limp, or a cane, or you have a seeing eye dog...Wait a minute...Forget the last one...If you have a seeing eye dog and you're driving, then fuck you!

Anyway, the point is, if you need the space, then I think most people, aside from parking lot attendants, will be fine with your parking there. Pregnant women, too, though many parking lots have special spots reserved for them as well.

If, however, you instead pull your Porsche into the handicapped area, claim two handicapped spots, leap out of your car like a whirling dervish and, dance your Bing Crosby Wannabe-ass into the WalMart while singing "It's Good to be Me" all while someone's 90-year-old Grandma is forced to walk from the end of the parking lot because, thanks to you, that's the only spot she could find? Well, you can betcha that your fantasy about being handicapped will be made a lot more real by the mob of angry shoppers waiting for you upon your return.

Handicapped Wannabees are also known as Scammers.

Hazardous Waste – People who think that turning on their hazard lights gives them license to park anywhere they want. Examples include

In the fire lane of a burning supermarket? Chill out, Buddy! I'll only be a minute and I got my hazards on!

In the middle of a narrow street in Manhattan on a Saturday afternoon? Chill out, Buddy! I'll only be a minute and I got my hazards on!

In the middle of the goddam road, at Costco, in between the gas pumps and the tire center (which, by happenstance, happens to be the only way out of this *Yuppy Motel*), while you wait for your husband to emerge from the sixth plane of hell with three shopping carts full of enough crap to feed Ethiopia for a week?

"CHILL OUT! I GOT MY HAZARDS ON!!!"

Using your hazards does not give you license to be an asshole. If it did, then the President of the United States would always have his hazards on.

Oh wait...Doesn't he...

Um...Bad example...

Chapter 5

Just park in a normal space like everyone else, OK?

Key Bait – If you are an asshole in a parking lot and then leave your vehicle unattended, you are *Key Bait*. People love to ruin the day of assholes, especially when they feel there are no consequences for doing so. Keys are cheap, but paint is expensive to replace. Lesson? **DON'T BE AN ASSHOLE!** *NOTE: It is VERY illegal to key or otherwise damage someone's car and if you are caught, you will probably go to jail, or at the minimum get your ass kicked.*

Mr. I'm So Special – People who park their motorized vehicles (usually motorcycles) in the pedestrian area of a shopping center, or even *inside the goddam store they're shopping at*. No, you're not special, unless you think being *Key Bait* is special. Then, you're all kinds of fucking special, Dickhead.

Murderous Shit For Brains – People who leave their pets in their cars while they shop, with the windows rolled up. Would you leave your kid in the car like this? If so, you are seriously in need of a visit from social services. The same goes for your dog, or your cat, or lizard, or whatever you claim to love but would still condemn it to a horrible and torturous death while you try on a new mu-mu. Leave Fluffy at home, or better yet, give her to someone who actually gives a shit about her. But don't bitch when I smash your window out to save her life.

Puffer Douche – That guy who, usually in parking lots, drives in the middle of the goddam lane. When he encounters you, he does not pull to the right, as that would require too much common sense. Instead, he just sits there and looks at you. He's like a puffer fish in that he's taking up as much space as possible in hopes that you will back up and find another way out of the parking lot.

What I like to do in these situations is pull right up to his bumper, shut off my car, and go inside as if nothing is wrong. Fuck him.

A Lesson in Ettiquette

Scammers – People who use the handicap spots when they are obviously not handicapped. I've seen teenagers borrow "grandma's" car for a quick trip to the mall and do this. Proof that not enough kids are getting spanked.
Note: Scammers are also known as "Handicapped Wannabees."

Sharks – In a crowded parking lot, these are other cars circling and trying to get a space.

Shit Out Of Luck – You are driving in a crowded parking lot with at least one car driving closely behind you. Just as you pass a minivan on your left, you see its reverse lights turn on. You stop your car, but you are too far past the space to get into it, and the guy behind you is too close for you to back up. He taps his horn. Translation? "You're shit out of luck, dude!"

Squacking – When two drivers are about to *Cross Swords*, but each is too proud to let the other person go first. So instead, they each lean on their horns and pull out into the aisle (and towards each other) in short, aggressive bursts.

Tailgators – People who stand (not in a car, but actually on their two feet) in a parking spot and wave off other cars because their "friend is on their way." The verdict is still out on whether or not these people fall into the "Asshole" category, since there are many situations where this is kosher, or even backed up by law[4]. All I know is that it sucks to be waved off of a space when you're circling downtown Baltimore, looking for a place to take a piss where you won't get killed in the process.

Thief – You are patiently waiting for someone to leave their spot. However, as they turn towards you as they leave, an asshole from the other

---

[4] In Baltimore, for example, when there is an excessive amount of snow, it is acceptable to reserve a space for yourself that you have shoveled out.

Chapter 5

direction speeds up and sneaks into the spot before you can get into it. This is why God made keys sharp and paint weak. You do the math.

NOTE: If you were just sitting there without your signal on, that space wasn't yours and the person who took it wasn't a *Thief*. You, however, are a dumb ass who is *Shit Out of Luck*.

Two-Time Losers – People who double park. How could anyone think this is acceptable? Apparently, these people do, and they obviously give about as much of a shit about traffic flow as I do about the paint on their car (see *Key Bait*). And no, putting your hazards on doesn't make this any more acceptable, Asshole.

Idiots in the Snow

In the time it took for you to find a spot in the WalMart parking lot, shuffle the kids into the store, wander the aisles looking for her hidden treasure, check out with said treasure, and load the kids back into the car again, the ground has become covered with over six inches of snow.

Hey, it could happen, right?

Moving on...

If you thought finding a spot in this maze was the apocalypse, now you are in the middle of a true-to-God uncensored display of Armageddon. Never before in the history of mankind has there been such a predictable breakdown in society than when soccer parent suburbanites from Richmond, VA see snow flakes (the kind that fall from the sky) and instinctively become compelled to stock up on bread and milk. Yes, bread and milk. I don't know what it is about bread and milk, but people go absolutely fucking nuts at the thought of being without bread and milk while there is snow on the ground outside. They descend on all grocery stores *en masse* like rodents fleeing the plague... except they are going *towards* the plague. Out *into* the snow. Because that makes sense.

Just like it makes sense that, because they all drive massive 4-wheel drive SUV's, they think they will be immune to the laws of physics...

At the time of this writing, my older son is eight years old. The other

Chapter 6

day, I asked him what he learned in school. He immediately lit up and asked, "Did you know that water freezes at 32 degrees Fahrenheit?"

"I did!" I said. I then asked him, "And what happens when you walk on ice?"

"You could fall down."

"And why is that?"

"Because ice is slippery."

"Is snow any less slippery than ice?" I asked.

"A little," he said. Then, he added, "But not really."

I thought about how funny it was that many people, upon entering their *Invincible Womb*, lose track of two very important laws of physics. Specifically, the laws that pertain to *Momentum*, and *Friction*. Friction is easy to take for granted because most of the time, most of us drive in above-freezing temperatures, during which friction keeps you from sliding into something and dying. But in a snow storm, the **lack** of *Friction* just baffles these stupid motherfuckers. It doesn't matter how many times they've driven in snow before, their focus on one mission –

"BREAD and MILK...BREAD and MILK...I have to get to the grocery store RIGHT NOW and buy BREAD and MILK..."

gives them leave of their senses. This *Fawkery* tends to increase the further south you go.

I.E. Places where it normally does not snow.

I've illustrated this phenomenon with this chart:

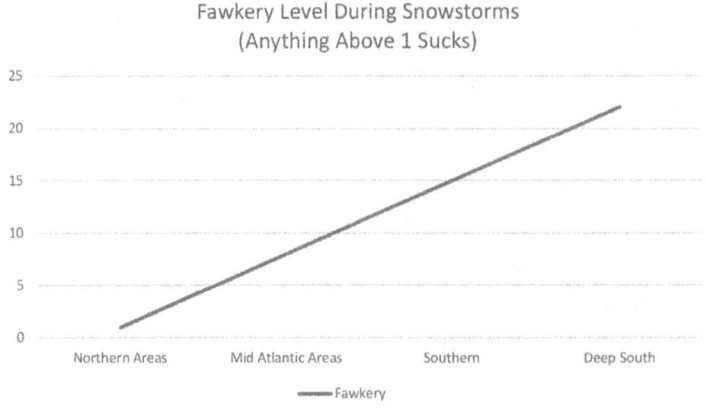

Idiots in the Snow

In Richmond, VA, it typically snows (and sticks to the roads) about once a year and the chaos that ensues is worse than a 12:05 in Times Square on New Year's morning. It's worse than 9pm on St. Patty's Day. It's like watching the climax of *The Gremlins*, with people and cars sliding this way and that, all in a panic

"MILK and BREAD . . . MUST HAVE MILK AND BREAD RIGHT FUCKING NOW!!!"

as if the end of the fucking world is approaching. And then, when you ask anyone in Richmond about how the roads are, they all seem to have the same answer:

"The roads are fine, but the drivers are idiots!"

Here's the thing about southern drivers in the snow. Because it snows so infrequently, rather than learn how to actually drive in the snow and ice, they buy a 4-wheel drive (or worse, an ALL-wheel drive) vehicle and think the problem is solved. Because, you know, the nice young man at the dealership told them they'd be ok.

HERE'S THE DEAL: Having a 4-Wheel Drive vehicle does not make you immune to the slippery characteristics of ice and snow. It may help you to get unstuck, or to get going from a stop, but the faster you are going, the less difference there is between you and a non-4-wheel drive vehicle.

Here's a graph to illustrate this mathematical certainty:

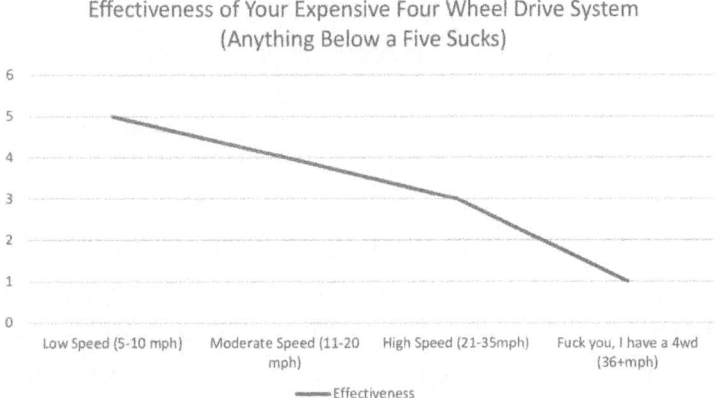

Chapter 6

By the way – "All-Wheel Drive" cars are even worse. What a bunch of nonsense, having a machine manage icy conditions when it cannot sense what's approaching. Perhaps this will change in the future, but at the time of this writing, only properly trained and managed **human** intelligence can predict and navigate less-than-ideal road conditions.

But I digress. This chapter is meant to define the various idiots that you may encounter in snowy conditions. The irony is that if you are a sensible *Good Driver*, you probably will never see one of these idiots, except on the news. Mainly because you won't be driving in the snow in the first place.

※ ※ ※

Braking – The worst possible fucking thing you can do while driving on snow or ice. Once you hit the brake, you are at the mercy of physics that are both completely outside of your control and reputably unsympathetic. Here's another way of putting it: You most likely will wind up on a YouTube video that uses the words "Darwinism" and "Traffic Fatalities" in the title. If you're in a snow storm, and you're going fast enough to think you may need to use your brake, then *Slow The Fuck Down* by *Coasting*, or by running into a tree before you fucking kill somebody. If you choose the latter, please undo your seatbelt first so as to improve the gene pool.

Bumper – A car stuck in the snow or on ice on the side of the road. Called such because if your car loses control, you may avoid *Sliding Off The Damn Road* by "bumping" into them. NOTE: If the disabled car is in the middle of the road, they are a *Landmine*.

Coasting – Slowing your vehicle by letting your foot off the gas (NOT *Braking*). If you try this under controlled conditions at home, you will notice that it takes a while to coast to a stop. Hopefully, your next instinct will be to not *Drive So Damn Fast* to begin with. Coasting is the proper way to avoid an accident, as opposed to *Braking*, which will most likely turn your car into a *Pinball*. See also *Slow The Fuck Down*.

Idiots in the Snow

Complete Lack of Sense – A driver who passes another vehicle anywhere on a snow-covered road. It doesn't matter if there are normally two lanes open on the road (and only one is snow plowed). It doesn't matter if you drive a 4-wheel drive, if you're from "New York City," if you have a *Fake ID*, or if you scored more than 120 on an online IQ test that Forest Fucking Gump could have passed while high. If you pass **ANYONE** who is moving (or about to move) **ANYWHERE** on a snow-covered road, you are a *Fucking Imbecile* who is displaying a *Complete Lack of Sense*.

Death – A state of permanent rest, punctuated by stiffening joints, bloating, flatulence, and overall rotting, followed by a compulsion by your relatives to bury or cremate you. In the USA in 2015, you had a .1% chance of experiencing death while in a motor vehicle, and this statistic rises every year. Please note that you can still be a *Good Driver* and experience *Death*, so watch out for the crazies. Including the one in your mirror.

Driving Too Damn Fast – If you're driving through snow (or on ice, through rain, etc), and your tires spin beyond traction, even just a little bit, you're *Driving Too Damn Fast*. By the way, your tires are more likely to spin when you are making a turn, so *Slow The Fuck Down* to avoid *Sliding Off The Damn Road*. I mean, WTF, Dude. Is that loaf of bread so goddam important that you'll risk the death not only of yourself, but of other people, too?

Fake ID – Someone from a southern state who claims that, because they've driven through New York once, they are as qualified to drive through snowy conditions as someone who's seen snow every day of winter since they were born. This would be like saying that someone from New York knows as much about trailer parks, tornado sirens, and aliens (the space kind) as someone from Arkansas. People know what they're surrounded with on a daily basis and no, you don't know how to drive in the snow, Fucktwat, because you've NEVER SEEN IT. And your *Fake ID* won't convince the officer you're anything other than a run of the mill *Jackass* who should have stayed at home. FUCK YOU!

Chapter 6

Friction – The resistance that one surface or object encounters when moving over another. Most relevant when driving in weather because the *lack* of friction, combined with *Driving Too Damn Fast* can cause *Gymnastics*, *Pinball*, *Fuckhole Orgies*, and *Death*.

Fuckhole Orgy – When a *Jackass* is the victim of someone scoring a *Touchdown* and subsequently slides into someone else. This chain reaction of incompetence is how Jack-Asses reproduce.

Gymnastics – The various twists, turns, and double-back flips that a vehicle does when it hits ice and loses control. Usually, the finale is a *Grand Slam*. See also *Pinball*.

Grand Slam – When multiple vehicles score *Touchdowns* at the same general time and location. To be a *Grand Slam*, the incident must involve 4 or more vehicles. I often carry judges signs with me so if I witness one of these, I can be the first one to rate their accident. "That's a solid 9, man!" or "Duuuuuuude! I'd give you a 10 if your kids had been decapitated – Nice work!" By the way, yes I know I'm mixing my sports references here. But I'd rather mix up sports terminology than my internal organs in a high speed crash, so *STFU* and listen. You may learn something.

Jackass – Anyone who drives around in the snow without damn good reason, and without the skills to do so. I don't care if you've been "cooped up with the kids all day." The only good excuse to leave the house in a blizzard is if you've run out of beer, AND HAVEN'T DRANK ANY YET. (Figure that one out and I'll give you a dollar.)

Land Mine – Someone whose car is stuck in snow or on ice, in the middle of a road. If they are on the side of the road, they are a *Bumper*.

Momentum – The quantity of motion of a moving body, measured as a product of its mass and velocity. In layman's terms, this means that your car is harder to stop when you are *Driving Too Damn Fast*, the threshold of which is lowered by the presence of snow and ice on the road.

Pinball – A car that spins out of control and hits more than one obstacle before scoring a *Touchdown*. Usually the result of *Driving Too Damn Fast* combined with a *Complete Lack of Sense*, followed by *Braking*.

Forward Rush – Driving WAY too fast for the conditions, motivated entirely by the hope of your momentum keeping you from getting stuck in the snow. Problem is, now you can't stop and you'll likely wind up scoring a *Touchdown*. Tell me something, Jerk Off. That snow plow mounted in the side of your face . . . Uncomfortable?

Royal Lane Mine – Someone whose car is stuck in the snow, in the middle of an intersection. This is the highest pinnacle of jackassedness that one can achieve. Bow and fall on your sword, Numnuts.

Sliding Off The Damn Road – What happens when someone with a *Complete Lack of Sense* is *Driving Too Damn Fast* and tries to make a turn. Whoops. Time to call Geico.

Slow The Fuck Down – Layman's term for decelerating, or what happens when you let your foot off the gas while driving on snow. If you try this under controlled conditions at home, you will notice that it takes a while to coast to a stop. Hopefully, your next instinct will be to not *Drive So Damn Fast* to begin with. Coasting is the proper way to avoid an accident, as opposed to *Braking*, which will certainly turn your car into a *Pinball*.

Snowball – A Volkswagen Beetle that has flipped onto its roof and is spinning from the momentum of its crash. Very rare, and a certain million hits on YouTube if you can video it . . . especially if you wreck your car trying to video it (and capture *that* on video).

Chapter 6

Tag – When a *Jackass* crashes into a *Land Mine* and inadvertently un-sticks the *Lane Mine*. It truly looks like a game of tag when the newly freed *Jackass*, who only a moment ago was a *Land Mine*, immediately crashes into someone else, thus creating two fresh new *Land Mines*. (See *Fuckhole Orgy*).

Touchdown – An accident that occurs because someone can't stop due to icy conditions. Four or more vehicles involved makes this a *Grand Slam*.

7

Communication

CASE STUDY

You stop at the traffic light and you hear a horn. You turn around, but there's no one there.

Then, you hear it again.

It's beside me.

You see the truck before you see the guy, because the truck has been lifted at least a foot and the shotgun seat's window of your car cuts off everything above the door handle. Just as you wonder why he's honking at you, he lowers his hand from the clouds and flips you an upside-down bird.

The Middle Finger. AKA, The Italian Salute.

"That boy flipped you off, Daddy." It's your son, from the back seat. Even at six, he understands profanity.

"Why did he flip you off?" Mademaoiselle asks.

"I have no idea," you say. And that's when you finally see him, through your sunroof.

Your son's description was perfect. He looks like he's about sixteen years old. His skinny face and skinny arms make him look even smaller against the backdrop of the monster truck he's driving than he probably is. He's wearing a baseball cap that advertises lawn mowers and over one ear, he carries a cigarette. His T-Shirt has a corpse printed on it. And his wiry and skinny fingers are adorned with cheap metallic rings.

He meets your eyes and mouths, *"You dumb fuck!"*

You turn away because the situation is ridiculous, but he simply hits

Chapter 7

his horn again. When you don't face him again, he leans on his horn. "Why is he honking at us, Daddy?"

"I don't know, Son," you say. "Just ignore him and he'll stop."

"You mean like my baby brother?"

"Yes," you say. "Ignore him like you would your baby brother."

But he doesn't go away. Instead, he just leans on his horn, demanding your attention as you count the seconds until the light turns green again...

We don't have many ways of expressing our displeasure at other folks' driving. Most people rely on a crude use of the horn and a few obscene gestures. What follows are several ways that drivers can use their horns and gestures to communicate with each other more effectively.

Method 1
The Horn Section

The horn is a masterpiece of communication. With one pitch, one timbre, and often with only one syllable, it transgresses all language barriers. No word in the English, or any other language, comes close to invoking the visceral reaction a horn creates. When you hear a horn, you'll usually snap to attention, wonder if it's you they're honking at, and then react.

Here are a few phrases that the horn can communicate in pretty much all areas of the world:

1. "Get the fuck out of the way!" (most common, applies to nearly every moment in traffic in New York City)
2. "What are you doing, Buddy?!" (someone stopping for no reason in front of you)
3. "The light's green, Jaggoff!" (someone doesn't go when they're supposed to)
4. "Get off your phone and drive!" (someone wandering into your lane)

5. *"Bon Pipe!"* (You're in your convertible on the highway and the trucker next to you toots his approval at the blonde head on your lap)

The horn was not designed to be polite. When you pound on it, you don't hear tweety birds and the gentle chimes of a baby mobile. You hear a sound that conveys the frustration of your soul ... the primal scream therapy you need after a day of eating shit from the boss ... the illusion of authority and control that you simply do not have ... the self-righteous indignation of dealing with yet another dumb fuck on the road ...

Or to just say, "Hi."

I'm usually embarrassed on the rare occasions a horn is blown at me. If I wasn't paying attention when the light turned green and someone reminds me with a horn, I'll typically go a little faster than I normally would have so they could make up the time. However, many people react with righteous indignation when a horn is blown at them. It doesn't matter if they were being a complete dumbass and almost killed you. If you hit the horn at them, they will be even dumber, more obstinate, and more deadly. (See *Self Righteous Douche*)

You know, just to show you that they meant to do it the first time.

Sigh.

It is because of this behavior, that I should probably cover how and when to use a horn. I wouldn't call it "Horn Etiquette," because as I've already pointed out, using a horn is, by its very nature, a rude thing to do. But sometimes you gotta be rude to get past the dumb asses that somehow got a license to operate a three ton hunk of rolling metal at lethal speeds through residential areas.

Situation 1
Traffic Light

You're at a light and it turns green. For whatever reason, the car in front of you doesn't move. Here's what you do next:

Chapter 7

1. Wait three seconds. This is more than enough time for them to notice the light has changed, take their foot off of the brake, and press the gas. Any less than three seconds and you're the asshole here.

2. *Tap* your horn. This will usually do the trick. They may even wave at you, which is essentially thanking you for halting their dumb-assedness. All is good in the world.

3. If, however, they don't notice the *Tap*, it's time to *Tap Twice / Double Tap*. I'll usually follow this up with going forward ever so slightly. They should definitely have a grasp on the situation by now. But if they don't...

4. Give 'em a *Two Second Blaat*. Keep in mind you are being very rude right now. Granted, they're *Stopping Up The Works* by sitting their fat ass in a lane that's supposed to go, but your rudeness could trigger them turning into a *Self-Righteous Douche*.

5. Lean on the horn and scream profanities about their mother. Who gives a shit at this point? Maybe he'll be a *Tough Guy* and get out of the car, which you can take as an opportunity to go around his dumb ass... Or better yet, run him over.

Disclaimer: You are NOT allowed to run people over, at least not in Virginia. In Brazil or Nigeria, perhaps, but not here.

Situation 2
Parking Lot

For whatever reason, you wind up waiting on some *Campers* to leave their spot.

You know that:

Communication

1. Hitting your horn at *Campers* will most often make them take longer to leave.
2. There are no other spots available right now, and there are a lot of *Sharks* circling.
3. You have to go to the bathroom really bad.

I have had more luck with waiting a polite amount of time and then knocking on their windows and politely asking them if they are leaving. Personally, I would see someone waiting for my spot and would feel the social pull to leave quickly, and I think most people would recognize that you're being polite and respectful.

Solution? Don't use the horn. Either wait for them to leave, however long it takes, or politely ask them if they are leaving.

Situation 3
The Wanderer

You're on the highway, cruising along in your lane (the right lane, I hope), when suddenly the guy in the lane next to you decides to start texting his mother. A moment later, his car starts to wander out of his lane and into yours.

1. A *Tap* isn't really enough here, and if you give him three seconds to correct the problem, you'll both be dead. Instead, immediately give him a *One Second Blaat*.
2. APPLY THE BRAKE! In a video game, the only penalty for a collision is hitting the reset button. But in REAL LIFE, and especially at HIGHWAY SPEEDS, the penalty for a collision is often death. Yes, it's idiotic and dangerous and crazy and your kids are in the car and *boy if I didn't have some place to be I'd get out of my car and teach you a lesson* ... But the fact of the matter is that if you hit the brake, the accident will not happen.

3. Once the situation has resolved itself (and if it's safe to do so), and you still feel your soul will forever crave satisfaction if you do nothing, pull up beside him and give him *The Look*.

Situation 4
Let's Go Back to High School

You're sitting at a red light when you see a girl you used to date a few cars away riding with some other dude. You hit your horn a few times to get their attention and when he turns around you give him the finger for a long time.

He shrugs and turns around, and you feel like an ass.

Then you realize you better get home before dusk or your Dad will take away the keys to your Trans Am for a week.

That's how this scenario *should* end, anyway. If, however, you're the type of complete fucking idiot who likes to showcase that you barely graduated high school by *getting out of your car to discuss the guy's driving "man to man?"* Then you are simply *asking* to go to jail.

But maybe that's exactly what you need. Who knows? In today's economy, it can be stressful to worry about when your next meal is going to come from, and prison alleviates you of that worry. I hear that some people get laid there, too, whether they like it or not.

Method 2
A Lesson in Morse Code

Not everyone knows Morse Code, obviously. But even if your intended audience doesn't understand what you're doing, it can still be fun to demonstrate intelligence in the face of idiocy. Morse is pretty easy, once you get the hang of it. A dash (_) means a longer horn duration than a dot (.). A space means a slight pause.

Here are some simple codes you can learn on your horn that actually spell out what you want to say to other drivers:

Communication

English	Morse
Hi!	.... ..
Thanks!	- .... .- -. -.- ...
BA (as in, "Back Atcha!")	-... .-
GOGI (as in, "Go On, Get In front of me.")	--. --- --. ..
Go (as in, "The light is green, Fucker!")	--. ---
MO (as in, "Move over.")	-- ---
No (as in, "Don't do that!")	-. ---
WTF (as in, "What the FUCK are you doing?")	.-- - ..-.
FU2 (as in, "Fuck You, Too!")	..-. ..- ..---
WTH (a more polite version of WTF)	.-- - ....
YM (as in, "Your Mother!")	-.-- --
GFY (as in, "Please exit the roadway so that you may pleasure yourself!")	--. ..-. -.--
NBJ (As in, "Mademoiselle is giving you a Nice blow job!")	-. -... .---

Please note that in many locales, it is illegal to honk your horn excessively. Make sure you know the local laws before using your horn to communicate in Morse Code.

Also please note that in most locales, it is illegal to give or receive a blow job while driving.

Chapter 7

Method 3
Sign Language

While the horn is one of the most effective ways of revealing your emotions to other drivers, it is not the most common means of doing so. Even people who are the least animated conversationalists in person will raise fingers and fists at their fellow drivers in protest of their being given licenses in spite of a complete lack of driving skills.

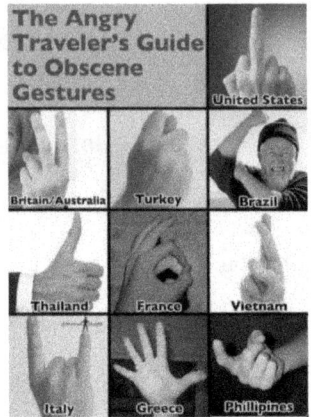

Literally EVERYONE is a born master of driver's side language. It's kind of like a slang tongue.

I miss a gesture? Email a pic to jjmcmoon@gmail.com!

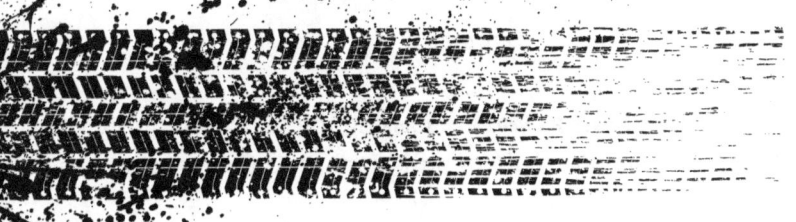

Aggressive Driving and Road Rage

CASE STUDY

Finally, you arrive at the mall.

Mademoiselle is happy. The kids are happy. And why wouldn't they be? They have zero responsibility, ultimate energy, and have you to save their lives every ten seconds from some hare-brained decision –

But I digress.

On the way into the mall, you see a family of four almost get run over by an SUV who just had to speed through the front Thruway in order to snag a front parking space. From your vantage point, it looked as though the kids would have been run over if the father hadn't yanked them out of the way without a second to spare.

You barely have a chance to discuss this with your wife when you see the father, who is clearly in "yanking" mode, walk over to the offending SUV, open the driver's door, and yank the driver out of his invincible womb. Actually, he doesn't really yank him out. The guy was getting out anyway and the father just helped him along. Some *Yuppy Pushing* ensues, accompanied by a bunch of awkward shouting. "Where do you get off driving like that?!" the father shouts.

"Where do you get off not diving out of the way fast enough?!" the driver retorts.

The whole thing looks really silly and the thought actually crosses your mind to stop and watch so that the kids can learn to laugh at such childish behavior. But just as you are passing the two rejects from the high school bully club, one of them pulls a gun and the comedy turns dramatic…

These days, it seems that just about everyone has their own definitions for *Aggressive Driving* and *Road Rage*. For the purposes of this book, these are the layman's definitions:

Aggressive Driving – Operating your motor vehicle up to and beyond its own mechanical limits and/or beyond the limits imposed by traffic laws. Examples of Aggressive Driving include:

1. Breaking the speed limit
2. Sudden and non-signaled lane changes
3. Tailgating
4. Swerving in and out of traffic in an attempt to "get there first."
5. Revving the engine at a traffic light in an attempt to bait other cars into racing, or bully them into letting you in front of them.

These aren't the only examples of Aggressive Driving, but you get the idea. If you're driving aggressively, you're basically treating the road as your own private NASCAR track, minus the fire-retardant suit, helmet, roll cage, and ambulance on standby.

Road Rage – Losing your temper behind the wheel to the point of unlawful aggression. Examples of Road Rage can include:

1. Overuse of your horn
2. Screaming and yelling at other drivers
3. Waving your fist and making other obscene gestures. Yes, flipping someone off is an act of *Road Rage*
4. Following (ie, Stalking) other drivers
5. Throwing items from your car at other cars (A felony in most states)

Aggressive Driving and Road Rage

6. Attempting to crash into "bad drivers," or run them off the road
7. Getting out of your car and confronting other drivers to "talk about" their driving like "men"
8. Waving a gun at, or actually shooting at, other drivers
9. Anything that causes fear or possible injury to another human being that isn't a reaction to *imminent harm to innocent human life*

It's important to note that *Aggressive Driving* is usually a traffic offense, while *Road Rage* is often criminal. To put it into perspective, if you are caught driving aggressively, you're usually given a summons and allowed to drive home. But if you're caught committing *Road Rage*, you're getting cuffed and thrown into jail. And not a nice jail, either. *Road Rage* isn't a white collar crime, so you won't be working on your back swing with the jet set. Instead, you'll be housed with big and hairy people who know a lot more about committing violent acts than you do, including (but not limited to) forcible sodomy, salad tossing, and anal rape.

Not sure what salad tossing is?

How about anal rape?

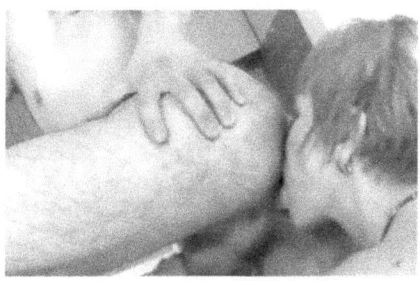

In case you're in doubt, you're the face in this picture

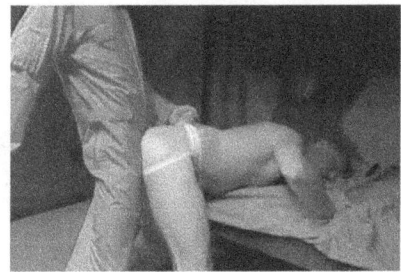

You're the *Catcher*, not the *Pitcher* in this photo

Chapter 8

Hmmmmmm . . . Suddenly, it's not so important to get to the Starbucks five minutes before everyone else, now is it?

So repeat after me:

No matter how badly someone else drives, I am not allowed to shoot them.

Let's say that again, just to be clear:

NO MATTER HOW BADLY SOMEONE ELSE DRIVES, I AM NOT ALLOWED TO SHOOT THEM.

And for the slower or newer members of the readership who need this to be a little clearer:

NO MATTER HOW BADLY SOMEONE ELSE DRIVES, IT IS NOT WORTH GETTING MY ASS CONSISTENTLY REAMED IN A COLD AND DARK SHITTY-SMELLING PLACE WHERE LIFE PERPETUALLY SUCKS AND NO ONE CARES.

While I have made jokes about *Road Rage* and other acts in this book, I'd like to point out that no one was shot in the writing of it. Please refer to the disclaimer on Page 1:

If you *Fuck Shit Up*, there are penalties that are designed to go well beyond your comfort zone.

This chapter is designed to both recognize and respond to acts of *Aggressive Driving* and *Road Rage* both in other drivers, and to recognize the temptation to engage in these behaviors yourself.

Part 1
What causes Aggressive Driving Behavior

If asked, most *Aggressive Drivers* would say that other drivers caused their own aggressive or violent behavior. But this is not true, and the failure to recognize that only accentuates the problem.

You and you alone are responsible for the emotions you experience, and the responses you have to those emotions.

Here is a scientific fact: If you experience a negative emotion, it only takes about 30 seconds for the chemicals behind that emotion to clear out of your brain and open up the opportunity to experience a different emotion. There are many self-improvement gurus out there who can help you manage this process, take control of your state of mind, and experience more positivity in your life. Those processes go beyond the scope of this book.

For now, just understand that it is your fault if you *Fuck Shit Up*.

It is **your** fault when you decide to execute a lane change at 80+ mph using the emergency lane to get around someone in the left lane.

It is **your** fault when you take your eyes off the road to scream and yell at someone who didn't use their turn signal... and then you rear end the car in front of you.

It is **your** fault when you decide to follow a "bad driver" to their house and then engage them with violence.

It is **NEVER** someone else's fault when you decide to shoot them because they drove in a way you didn't like.

Understanding that you are responsible for what you do is the first step. The second step is dealing with your emotions in a productive (or at least non-criminal) manner. Here are some scenarios and techniques that have worked for me, and hopefully will at least inspire you to stay out of prison.

Part 2
How to Avoid Driving Aggressively

1. **Take a few deep breaths.** Yes, this idea feels cliché, but it works. Here's why: Firstly, it takes about 30 seconds to do this and we've already established that it only takes that long to clear out a negative emotion from your brain. But it also works because the influx of more oxygen is relaxing, which swings the pendulum away from the intensity that all negative emotions have in common. You'll find after you do this, what just infuriated you won't matter so much anymore.

Chapter 8

2. **Put the situation into perspective.** Yes, it is "driving you nuts" that the Prius driver in front of you is *Holding Hands* with the minivan in the right lane and won't let you pass. But will shooting him really make your situation better? I guarantee that if you answered yes to this (hopefully rhetorical) question, you will change your mind real quick once Bubba pops your cherry in the Big House. It ain't worth it, Bro. The Prius will be out of your life sooner than the memory of Bubba's Big Penis, believe me.

3. **Get out of the game.** Ask yourself why it's so important to go faster? Is there a prize if you get to the mall first? Do they give you a free fucking toaster or something? Most likely not. So why not just get into the right lane, set your cruise for a mile or two less than the flow of traffic, and chill? Turn on your favorite playlist and laugh at how angry all of the other drivers are getting at that Prius. Who knows? Maybe someone else will shoot him.

4. **Venting** – While technically, this is borderline *Road Rage* in itself, I find little harm in talking to yourself when the stress of being trapped behind a *Blockade* or in stop and go traffic in a sea of *Merge Morons* becomes overwhelming. As long as no one else hears you, and you remain focused on the road, *Venting* out loud can help relieve this stress, and can even help you to laugh at the situation. **Warning:** Be careful not to fuel the fire when you do this. If you start off talking about the other drivers, and then escalate to shouting at them, it's time to try something else. Like deep breaths, for example. Trust me – it works!

As of this writing, the NHTSA reports at over 66% of traffic fatalities are a result of aggressive driving and 37% of Aggressive Driving incidents involve a firearm. [5] Over the past seven years, it's been estimated

---

5 http://www.safemotorist.com/articles/road_rage.aspx

that over 200 murders have been associated with *Road Rage*.[6] Just think about that for a second... People are actually *shooting each other* because they don't like how they drive. In any other situation in life, a normal person would simply know that this behavior is unacceptable, but in the *Invincible Womb*, a violent response somehow feels justified. Trust me, it isn't. You'll do the same time for a *Road Rage* incident that you would if you decided to shoot someone anywhere else. Possibly more.

Yes, I realize that this book was written largely in response to bad drivers on the road, but I'd like to point out that no one was shot in the making of this book.

Please take responsibility for your own emotional management and for your own actions. The consequences far outweigh any momentary gain you may think you'll experience.

Part 3
How to Deal With Aggressive Drivers

When someone is driving aggressively, or exhibiting angry behavior, most people feel the need to make them angrier. I'm not sure why that is, though I have to admit that I feel it myself. Someone's tailgating me when I'm in the left lane? I'll feel like staying in the left lane. Someone hits their horn at me? I'll feel like honking back. Someone is weaving in and out of traffic behind me? I'll feel like blocking their path. Screw them, right? Why should I indulge in their tantrum?

The fact is that we live in a civilized society where the justice system is supposed to catch these guys in the act and discourage their behavior or take them off the road entirely. It's not up to us to be *Vigilantes*. More to the point, by choosing to be a *Vigilante*, you are no longer an *innocent human life*, which is the standard necessary for a self-defense claim.[7]

---

6   http://brandongaille.com/21-startling-road-rage-facts-and-statistics/
7   I am not a lawyer, and this book is not a legal reference. It is strongly recommended that you contact an attorney before making any decisions suggested by or otherwise alluded to in this book. Saying that this book justifies your engaging in criminal behavior will NOT be an acceptable defense in a courtroom.

Chapter 8

So let's play this out. You're in the left lane, passing someone in the right lane. Suddenly, a *Terrorist* gets on your ass and starts flashing his lights. It is obvious that he feels that you aren't passing fast enough, but you decide to teach him a lesson and slow down. You create a *Blockade* and to further fuck with him, you flip him off. When that doesn't get him to ease off you, you tap your brakes, maybe even suddenly, which almost causes him to rear end you.

After a while, you get bored and finish the pass. You pull into the right lane and decide that the situation is over. Except the *Terrorist* hasn't forgotten about you, or how much of an asshole you just were to him. He pulls alongside you and throws a half-full *Double Gulp* soft drink (or worse) at you, causing you to crash your car and lose the ability to walk without a limp. Or worse.

Do you feel like a winner now? Make no mistake. It was a felony for him to do that, but who's in the hospital? He or you? If they even catch the guy, his prison sentence or insurance claim will do nothing to make it easier for you to piss standing up again.

Let's take this a step further. Let's assume that he doesn't throw the *Double Gulp*, but instead pulls a gun on you. Is his "being wrong" going to do anything to give you your life back?

To take this another step further, let's say you have a gun, also. You view this as an opportunity to use it, when in fact you will do as much time as he will because you contributed to escalating the situation. And even if you didn't, the way the criminal justice system in 'Merica works, you will spend much money and much time and much stress and much much more than it was worth bothering with to defend lawsuits and criminal charges for firing a gun from your vehicle on a motorway. And that doesn't even take into account the possibility of hitting an innocent bystander.

This book isn't a lesson in legal recourse, and I'm not going to debate your rights to shoot someone in self defense. All I'll say is that the trouble you'll go through for going down that road will be far greater than just getting out of the *Terrorist's* way to begin with. You may feel a little deflation of the ego, but I'll take that over a massive deflation of my wallet or freedom anyday, Dig?

Aggressive Driving and Road Rage

So what follows are some strategies for avoiding the dangers of *Aggressive Drivers*, and in turn, avoiding becoming a victim of *Road Rage*.

Part 4
How to avoid becoming a victim of Road Rage

1. **Don't drive like an asshole.** This is the absolute best thing you can do to avoid becoming a victim of *Road Rage*. When you started this book, you probably recognized the drivers I've described as *other people*, right? Now that you're nearing the end, hopefully you've seen a little of yourself as well. So let me ask you a straight up question: Do you drive like an asshole? What are you doing behind the wheel that may make someone want to shoot you?

   Here's a case study of this. I was visiting friends in Denver, Colorado and in my time there, I encountered some of the most dangerous and aggressive drivers I've ever seen in the United States. Over the course of a single weekend, I personally witnessed dozens of *Terrorists* and *Stalkers*, and saw at least two people get out of their vehicles to confront drivers at traffic lights. They must not have many police in Colorado, or at least not ones who pay attention to aggressive driving.

   Anyway, I was on a normal road with two lanes going in each direction. Because my GPS was telling me that I was going to make a left soon, I was in the left lane. Sure enough, a *Terrorist* got on my tail and not only started flashing his brights, but also leaned on his horn.

   I knew that he didn't realize that I was making a left soon, because I wasn't close enough to that turn to put my signal on. He probably also didn't realize that I wasn't from the area and felt it was safer to be in the left lane at that point in my journey than to pull an *Oh Yeah* and get into the left lane at the last minute. My emotional gut reaction to his behavior was to get pissed, but I'd be lying if I said my adrenaline wasn't pumping, too. The fight-or-flight response is involuntary.

   Rather than engage in aggressive behavior myself, I simply didn't

Chapter 8

change anything about what I was doing. I knew I was making a left soon and the situation would sort itself out. But that wasn't enough for this guy. Before I ever got to my turn, the guy used the right turn lane to get around me . . . and then slammed on his brakes when he was barely in front of me. I don't know how I missed him, except to say that the stopping distance of my rental Malibu must be less than the monster truck he was driving. I got into the right lane, not caring so much anymore that I would miss my turn. At this point, the inconvenience of circling a block to get back onto my route (or following an alternate route on my GPS) was minor compared to whatever this crazy fuck was willing to do in order to prove that his penis isn't, in fact, the size of a Vienna sausage (no matter what his Mom says). It also turned out that that guy was making a left where I wanted to, so he basically risked his life, and mine, and however many other innocent bystanders may have been involved if we had crashed, in order to first get to the red light 100 feet away.

Let me say that another way: His "prize" in all this was to wait ten feet closer to the intersection than he would have been if I had gotten there first.

The point of this story is to keep in mind that the road is not all about you. Everyone has a story and because we can't communicate with the spoken word to each other while we're driving (even with sign language and Morse Code), intentions can be misread. For all I know, his wife was in the backseat giving birth. Or his father was in the car passing a kidney stone on the way to the hospital.

Or his inbred little boy asked him how he, too, could be a redneck and it was a teaching moment.

The point is, you don't know and neither did I. I circled the block and got back on my route and never saw him again.

1. **Avoid the situation.** In the example above, I deviated from my route to avoid the encounter, but most often you don't even need to do that. Just get into the right lane and go slower than they are going. Unless you just ran over their child, they'll quickly realize that there are other drivers to pass and they'll forget all about you.

Aggressive Driving and Road Rage

2. **Don't engage the aggressive driver.** If you even look at them, you may add fuel to the fire. Remember – You don't know what their story is. They could have just gotten fired or could have a severely bleeding child in the back seat. Just get out of the way and pay attention to what you're doing.

3. **If they don't leave you alone, CALL THE COPS.** Remember this if nothing else: The cops are there to help you. If you go waving a gun around, the cops won't listen to a word you say and will shoot you if you don't stop it. Call 911 and tell them what's going on. Give them the description of the car, including license plate number, and tell them where you are.

4. **DO NOT STOP YOUR VEHICLE.** If someone is stalking you, avoid an area with traffic lights and stop signs. Gas stations are not safe places, and neither are shopping malls. A police station would be a good place to go, as would a hospital's emergency entrance. Just remember, if you did anything illegal to piss off the other driver, you will be prosecuted for it, so again *DON'T BE AN ASSHOLE!*

5. **Install a Car Camera.** Note that I don't mean, "Turn on your iPhone to video mode and press record and point it at the aggressive driver." Not only is this illegal in most states (Refer to your states' "Hands-Free Driving" laws to be sure), but it is more likely to antagonize the aggressor than it is to ward them off. Also, it'll distract you from your own driving and you could get into an accident with someone else. What I'm talking about are the car cameras that you can install on your rear view mirror or bumper (or other safe place) that will automatically record what's going on so you have it later. Keep in mind that this will document what **actually** happened, so make sure that you weren't driving like an asshole. And no, you most likely won't have a chance to edit the video so again, make sure you weren't driving like an asshole.

Don't Be A Dick!

Epilogue

With a practiced smile, you walk with the family through a sea of grim strangers who are fighting for the same shiny and useless crap that you are. You are a dutiful pack mule. Your biceps burn, and you know that Mademoiselle will bitch about getting five cents on the dollar (if that) on all of it at the HOA garage sale next spring, but you'll deal with that later.

For now, she's happy.

All is good.

With arms aching, it's finally time to find the car. The gunslingers are gone, and no one tries to run you and your family over as you're exiting the parking lot. You walk up the aisle towards your SUV and no *Sharks* creep up on you.

And, after you load all of the boxes and bags and kids and wife into the SUV and take your seat behind the wheel, you are filled with a sense of calm.

A moment of silence passes.

And then another.

Breathe in ... Breathe out ...

"Are you going to start the engine, Daddy?"

You take another breath. "Yes, Son," you say and you push the button. But you don't put the SUV into Drive just yet. The engine is hypnotic, soothing, relaxing. It's the first moment of calm you have had all day long.

"Honey, let's go home," Mademoiselle says with a gentle touch on your arm.

You turn to her and smile. You program the GPS, not because you don't know the way home, but for its countdown of miles and minutes.

Epilogue

"You are 12 miles from your destination," it says. "You should arrive in 15 minutes."

"Yeah, right," you say and pull out of the parking space...

Just as a little dude driving a two decade old Corvette flies by you at aircraft speed, nearly taking off your bumper. "FUCK YOU!" the driver screams with his middle finger extended. The pitch of his voice lowers from the Doppler effect as he careens around a corner.

The shot of adrenaline makes you feel like your heart is going to explode out of your chest. You take a deep breath and ask, "Is everyone OK?"

"Yes, Daddy," your sons answer, almost in unison.

After a moment, you look at the GPS again.

You are 12 miles from your destination.

"We've got to do it all over again," you say.

"What was that?" Mademoiselle asks.

You smile. "Nothing," you say as you ease your foot off the brake.

Cautiously, you begin the ride home.

www.ingramcontent.com/pod-product-compliance
Lightning Source LLC
LaVergne TN
LVHW011206080426
835508LV00007B/634